EVALUATING TRAINING

EVALUATING TRAINING

A resource for measuring the results and impact of training
on people, departments and organizations

**Sharon Bartram and Brenda Gibson
of SBG Associates**

Gower

© SBG Associates 1999

The materials that appear in this book, other than those quoted from prior sources, may be reproduced for education/training activities. There is no requirement to obtain special permission for such uses.

This permission statement is limited to reproduction of materials for educational or training events. Systematic or large-scale reproduction or distribution – or inclusion of items in publication for sale – may be carried out only with prior written permission from the publisher.

Published by
Gower Publishing Limited
Gower House
Croft Road
Aldershot
Hampshire GU11 3HR
England

Gower
Old Post Road
Brookfield
Vermont 05036
USA

Sharon Bartram and Brenda Gibson have asserted their right under the Copyright, Designs and Patents Act 1988 to be identified as the authors of this work.

British Library Cataloguing in Publication Data
Bartram, Sharon
   Evaluating training : a resource for measuring the results
and impact of training on people, departments and
organizations
   1.Employees – Training of – Evaluation
   I.Title II.Gibson, Brenda
   658.3'12'404

ISBN 0 566 07805 8   Looseleaf
     0 566 08196 2   Hardback

Library of Congress Cataloging-in-Publication Data
Bartram, Sharon.
   Evaluating Training : a resource for measuring the results and
impact of training on people, departments and organizations /
Sharon Bartram and Brenda Gibson
      p.   cm.
   ISBN 0-566-08196-2. – ISBN 0-566-07805-8 (binder)
   1. Employees – Training of – Evaluation. I. Gibson, Brenda.
II. Title.
HF5549.5.T7B2919   1999
658.3'12404 – dc21   98-32253
                                                                                               CIP

Typeset in 12pt Palatino by Wearset, Boldon, Tyne and Wear and printed in Great Britain by MPG Books Ltd, Bodmin.

Contents

Preface vii
Introduction ix

PART ONE   THE EVALUATION AUDIT 1

Introduction 3
1 A quick assessment 5
2 Guidance notes 7
   Organizational culture 7
   The value of training 10
   Readiness for learning 12
   The purpose of evaluation 14
   Evaluation strategy 16
3 Audit action plan 19

PART TWO   THE INSTRUMENTS 23

Introduction 25
A **Measuring results** 29
   Introduction 29
   Index of instruments 31
   Checklist 33
1 Training needs analysis 35
2 The training needs process 39
3 Training methods 43
4 Training design 47
5 Learner feedback 51
6 Interest and involvement 59
7 Coaching 63
8 Instructing 67
9 Trainer style 71
10 Trainer profile – self-assessment 75

11	Trainer profile – learner assessment	81
12	Outcome assessment	87
13	Practical assessment	95
14	Learner self-assessment	101
15	Learner reactions	107
16	What have you learned?	109
17	Presenting group learning	113
18	Learning summary	115
B	**Measuring impact**	**119**
	Introduction	119
	Index of instruments	121
	Checklist	122
19	Draw a picture	123
20	Quantifiable evidence	127
21	Write a story	133
22	Open-ended statements	137
23	Learning journal	141
24	Impact questionnaire	149

Preface

Evaluating training sounds as though it should be straightforward. You want to know to what degree your training has worked and how this will change what happens in your organization. Working with a variety of clients has shown us that putting evaluation into practice is anything but straightforward. Just getting other people interested can be a battle in itself and perhaps you have other priorities that limit your time for this key element in the training cycle.

We would say that if you are not evaluating training then you are missing the best opportunity you have for making your training count.

Can we help you to make evaluation easier so that it is not neglected? We think so, and we have set out to produce a manual that offers you practical and creative ways of measuring the results and impact of training. It will help you to take stock of all the stages in your training and, by using the instruments, activate the changes you want your training to achieve.

We say what we mean by evaluation and show you that evaluating training is more than just a good idea; it is a vital part of the training process. Evaluation is the continual improvement programme for all your training, with the added benefit of helping to embed the learning into the working process.

Evaluation is not just an add-on to a training programme; it is an integral part that needs to be considered right at the beginning of your plans for development. It need not be difficult – in fact it can provide stimulation and focus to help you create training programmes that really do what they set out to.

We have developed the techniques in this manual with all of this in mind and they have been tried and tested in a variety of business settings. We hope we can inspire you to take a fresh look at evaluation as you try them out.

Sharon Bartram and Brenda Gibson

SGB Associates

Introduction

If you see training as the catalyst for change in how people do things, then a way to look at evaluating training is to see it as the means of activating the change. By measuring the results achieved by training, in other words the learning that has taken place, and also measuring the impact of this on people, departments, customers, the business and so on, you can help people to change their everyday routines. Eventually, the more you train and evaluate the training, the more likely you are to create an environment where learning is a natural part of everyone's routine.

Evaluation is often neglected or done in a piecemeal way. Perhaps the reason for this lies in how evaluation is sometimes perceived: a search for a scientific truth about the outcomes of training and the value of this to organizations. This can seem a hard thing to do and a thankless task, especially if no one is interested in the findings. It does not have to be like this; the key is to recognize evaluation for what it is. It involves you, the learners and others, gathering evidence to show whether learning has taken place and to what extent this has changed the way that things are done. The evidence may be quantifiable from practical tests, organizational indicators and so on, but it will also be qualitative, from people's perceptions, feelings and attitudes about the training. By comparing the evidence you will know whether the learning has been transferred into everyday routines and so has had an impact on the organization.

When we talk about evaluating training, then, we mean two things:

- *measuring results* – to determine the degree of learning that has taken place; and
- *measuring impact* – of the results on the people involved, their departments and ultimately the organization.

This manual provides a variety of techniques to realize the full potential of evaluating training. It is more than a collection of forms – yes, some of the instruments do use a form to gather information, but there are many which include handouts to help you get the best from the activity described.

In Part One, The Evaluation Audit, we encourage you to take a step back and carry out an audit of what you do. You will find background information on the key elements that affect evaluation, as well as the means to assess your current practice and to create action plans for the future. There is an outline audit action plan for you to record your findings and actions.

We begin Part Two, The Instruments, with an introduction explaining the range of instruments and giving guidance about winning the commitment and support of others to the evaluation process. There is an outline planning form to enable you to work effectively with the instruments.

We have arranged the instruments themselves into two sections. The first, Measuring results, gives you a range of ready-to-use materials that generate both quantifiable and qualitative evidence so that you can answer the question: 'What have people learned from the training?' Using the instruments will put you in a position to determine the degree of learning that has taken place. There is guidance on how to analyse and compare the information you gather so that you can draw conclusions about the results of the training, and how to encourage the transfer of learning into the workplace.

In the second section, Measuring impact, you will find more ready-to-use materials and guidelines for creating your own instruments to check effects of the training. In other words, you will be able to answer the question: 'People have learned to do things differently or do new things, so what difference has this made to them, their department and the organization?' The instruments will generate both quantifiable and qualitative evidence about how things are before and after the training. There is guidance on how you can analyse this information, draw conclusions and report your findings.

In both sections of instruments we have left to you the decision about asking people to identify themselves. We would encourage people to take responsibility for what they say, but having a space for names on any forms does eliminate that choice. We suggest you weigh up each situation and negotiate with those involved.

Whether you are new to evaluation or an 'old hand', we think there is something in the manual for you. You can use it in a number of ways:

- as an opportunity for personal development;
- to kick-start evaluation when you are not sure how to go about it;
- to bring a fresh perspective to what you already do to evaluate training.

It will be well worthwhile working through Part One to get a sense of what is happening around you before you embark on using the instruments from Part Two to help you activate the changes your training has generated.

PART ONE

The evaluation audit

Introduction

How do you evaluate training? What support do you have for this in your organization? If you don't evaluate training but see the need to, how do you start?

The Evaluation Audit will help you to answer these and many other questions about evaluating training so that you can assess the effectiveness of your current strategies. It will help you to recognize where you need to make changes as well as giving you guidelines for what to do if you are starting from scratch.

The audit is made up of three components, organized into three sections:

1. A quick assessment against the factors involved in evaluating training.
2. Guidance notes on carrying out an audit of each factor: what to find out, methods for doing this, possible consequences on evaluation and actions to consider.
3. An action plan that enables you to record the outcomes of your audit and the actions you and others will take in the future.

To get the best from the audit, start by completing the quick assessment. This will enable you to identify the priority areas to work on in your organization. Then refer to the guidance notes to plan your audit. Finally, audit your priority areas using the action plan to record actions for you and others to take in the future.

You could, of course, decide that all the factors need consideration, as one is likely to have a bearing on another. If this is the case, use the assessment to show you where your strengths and weaknesses are and then work through the guidance notes in sequence. These will help you to plan your audit. Again, you can use the action plan to summarize your findings and identify actions for you and others to take in the future.

1

A quick assessment

Each of the questions that follow relates to the key elements that affect the evaluation of training. To identify your priorities, or strengths and weaknesses, decide whether you can answer YES or whether you have to answer NO or IN SOME WAYS. Be as candid as you can.

		YES	NO	IN SOME WAYS
1	Does the culture of our organization help the process of evaluation?			
2	Do we work in an environment where training is valued?			
3	Do we work in an environment where there is readiness for learning?			
4	Do we have a clear purpose for evaluating training? 4.1 Do we involve the right people in our evaluation? 4.2 Do those involved have a clear understanding of their role and responsibility in evaluation? 4.3 Do we use the results obtained from our evaluation? 4.4 Do we report the results of our evaluation?			
5	Do we have a clear evaluation strategy that is understood by everyone? 5.1 Does our strategy enable us to measure the effectiveness of our: ● Training needs analysis process? ● Training design, content and methods? ● Trainer style? ● External provision? 5.2 Do we put resources aside to carry out evaluation effectively?			

If you have answered mainly YES to the questions, then your audit should show that your evaluation is working well. If you have answered mainly NO, you can use the audit to help you and others tackle evaluation. If you have answered mainly IN SOME WAYS, you can use the audit to build on your success and make your evaluation even more effective.

Refer to the guidance notes that follow to help you to plan your audit. The notes relate to the five areas covered by this assessment.

2
Guidance notes

Organizational culture
The way an organization works is a good indicator of how seriously it takes, or is likely to take, the evaluation of training. Take a look at your organization:

What to audit	*How to audit*
Forward planning Do we have plans about goals and objectives? Do these plans take into account how our people will be affected? Do these plans help us to identify and prioritize our training needs?	Compare current training activity to goals and objectives to find out if there is a correlation between them.
Communicating information Does everyone in the organization know about the goals and objectives? Do they understand how these affect the way they do their jobs?	Review the literature produced in the organization, for example newsletters, annual reports and so on. Ask people throughout the organization for feedback, using a questionnaire or face-to-face interviews.
Feedback Is feedback encouraged? Are there formal and informal mechanisms in place for giving feedback? Is feedback acted upon or ignored?	Review the systems and processes operating in the organization. Ask people throughout the organization for their opinions, using a questionnaire or face-to-face interviews.

The culture of an organization will affect the evaluation of training in a number of ways. An audit of this aspect should help you to determine the type of culture that predominates in your organization and the potential consequences for any evaluation strategy you may already have or try to develop in the future. After completing your audit, decide if your organization is uncoordinated or coordinated. Read the descriptions that follow and decide where you would place your organization on the continuum between the two types. Place crosses on the dotted lines to indicate your perceptions.

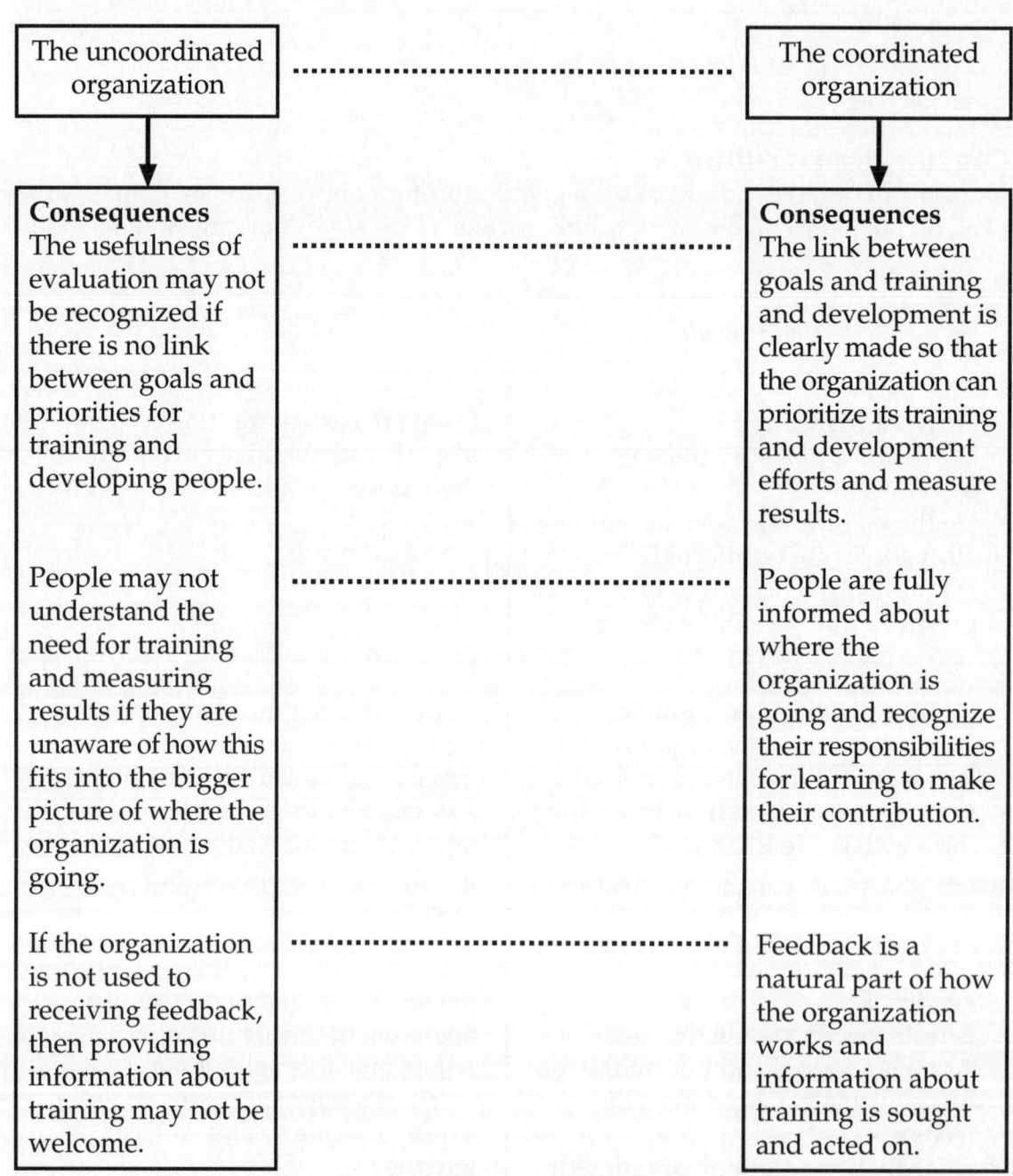

Here are examples, which highlight the differences between everyday practice in an uncoordinated and coordinated organization:

> We came across an organization that on the face of it supported the training and development of its people. A series of workshops was commissioned on an aspect that the training manager had been assured was a priority. The workshops began and immediately delegates were withdrawn by their managers because of pressures of work. Ultimately the workshops were postponed when questions were asked about their relevance to the business at that time. It was impossible to get agreement to the evaluation of the training, again because of perceived time problems and the lack of relevance to the business. There were 'happy sheets' at the end of the workshops and these indicated that the training had been useful, but without a fuller evaluation the extent of learning and the impact of this in the workplace would go unknown. A truly uncoordinated organization!
>
> Another organization set up its training based on the business plans for various business units. Managers had the responsibility of working with their people to identify delegates for courses that covered both technical and interpersonal skills. As well as the trainer, who was the main course tutor, a representative from the management team would attend and take part in running the programmes. There were no instances of delegates being withdrawn at short notice and the learning was evaluated by the managers in the workplace through observation and feedback. They regularly reported on the effects of the training on their business units and, from this feedback, the course portfolio was updated. Organizations can be coordinated sometimes.

If your findings show that your organization has more in common with the uncoordinated type, then you may have further groundwork to do before you and others can benefit fully from evaluating training. Some actions to consider are:

- Find others who support your ideas about evaluating training and ask for their help to influence and persuade key decision makers.
- Find other organizations which most closely match the coordinated type and use these as case studies to support any proposals for change.
- Show people the benefits of evaluation. In other words, tell them what they would gain and build up evidence from a training event to support your ideas.

The value of training

Take stock of the way people are trained and developed in your organization:

What to audit	*How to audit*
Making training count Do managers make the link between organizational objectives and training needs? Do managers support the need to train and develop people? Do managers accept that they have a role in making training work? Is time given to identifying and analysing training needs in an objective way?	Ask people throughout the organization for feedback, using a questionnaire or face-to-face interviews. Review the systems that exist to highlight training needs, such as appraisals, and assess the quality and accuracy of the information generated. Work with others to review recruitment practice – are people with the necessary skills recruited rather than existing people trained? Ask people who leave the organization about their experiences of being trained.
Training provision Is training provided for all or some people? Are people rewarded for undertaking training? Are time and resources made available for training?	Review current training activity and compare to training activity one year ago to assess what is provided and for whom. Track the career history of a sample of people at all levels to determine any links between their progress and training. Review current training budgets and compare to previous years to assess the level of financial support available.

If training is perceived as having value, the positive effects on evaluation are likely to be:

- A willingness to find out how effective the training has been and the changes it has made.
- The creation of an environment of continuous improvement where people are encouraged to build on their learning; information about results and impact becomes an integrated part of this process.

- A commitment to giving time and effort for people to learn and so a desire to know that this has a positive effect on everyday routines and organizational success.

If there is no perceived value to training, there will be a corresponding negative effect on evaluation:

- There is unlikely to be much training activity to evaluate.
- People will work to maintain their perception and so place barriers in the way of training.
- There will be little or no interest in the outcomes of any training.

Again, you may find that your organization falls somewhere between these two extreme positions. For example, you may find that people say they value training but have difficulty in making the most of it. They may quote time constraints, pressure of work and so on as reasons for not carrying through what they know to be a good thing. A situation that we met illustrates this:

> A company was introducing new computer systems and, three weeks before going 'live', they realized that some staff would need training. The training department was hastily brought in to arrange something. A course was put together but because of a breakdown in communications between the managers (they thought they had done their job just by asking for training and did not become involved any further) and the trainers, some people did attend whilst others did not. By the time the system was up and running there were still people who did not have the key skills. The training was blamed for not achieving results.

Some actions to consider in changing perceptions about training are:

- Find other organizations that do value training and use these as case studies to support your ideas.
- Involve managers in the process of analysing training needs.
- Start a dialogue with managers about issues they want to see resolved and work with them to decide how training can contribute to this and what is their part in making it work.

Readiness for learning

What about the people involved in training activities? Find out about their attitudes towards training and learning:

What to audit	*How to audit*
Identifying training needs Do people have a say in determining their own training needs? Do people have a say in determining how they will learn, whether new things or how to do things differently?	Ask people throughout the organization for feedback, using a questionnaire or face-to-face interviews. Review the systems that exist to highlight training needs, such as appraisals, and assess the quality and accuracy of the information generated.
Learning Do people perceive any benefits to them from learning? Do people perceive that they will be able to put learning into practice in their workplace? Do people willingly participate in training activities or do managers coerce them into taking part?	Ask people throughout the organization for feedback, using a questionnaire or face-to-face interviews. Compare the number of people nominated for training to the number who actually attend. Monitor the reasons given by people for not attending training.

Without readiness for learning the results of any evaluation will be skewed. This happens because people do not know why they are being trained and often take it as a criticism, an indication that in some way they are not up to scratch. Also, people may find the training useful but say that they cannot change what they do at work because of their manager. The following situation illustrates this point:

> The MD of a company thought it would be a good idea if the first line managers improved their leadership, teambuilding and communication skills. The MD commissioned a series of workshops on these topics and the first line managers had the chance to select the ones they wanted to attend. The workshops went ahead but had a high drop-out rate. When questioned, the participants said that they could not see the point of the training; their managers had not been involved in any of the planning and thought it was all a waste of time. This perception affected the participants, who felt they would be spending time on training that they would not use.

Some actions you can take to influence people's readiness for learning are:

- Involve people in the process of identifying and analysing training needs.
- Encourage dialogue between people and their managers so that the benefits of training can be determined between them.
- Coach people in learning to learn.

The purpose of evaluation

Here is an example that we have come across:

> A fairly large organization had a training function of three people. The trainers provided a range of training courses throughout the year for people at all levels in the organization. The evaluation of the training was limited to a comment sheet issued at the end of each course. When the trainers were asked about this they said that this was all the information they wanted to know. Their purpose for evaluation was to get good reactions to the courses so that they could argue for more staff and run even more courses. This focus on inputs, rather than outputs, meant that this organization could have been involved in training activity that was not bringing about change to the way people did their jobs. They would not know this because the evaluation undertaken was not measuring results or impact, only reactions to the training events themselves.

Consider the purpose of evaluating training in your organization:

What to audit	*How to audit*
Purpose Can we describe our reasons for evaluating training? Do we have a common purpose for evaluating training or are we working to different agendas? Does our purpose remain constant or are we driven by different training situations?	Check written policies on training and development to find out if a purpose has been made explicit. Ask those involved what the purpose is and compare the responses to see if there is a shared understanding. Compare different training interventions to assess the appropriateness of the evaluation undertaken.
Focus Do we intend our evaluation to focus on inputs or outputs? Does our practice match this?	Review information gathered from different training interventions to determine what has been measured. Review methods used to gather information to determine if they do find out what is intended.
Involvement Do others get involved in evaluating training, e.g. managers, learners? Do others know why they are involved and the benefit of this to making the training work?	List the people involved in recent evaluations. Ask people throughout the organization for feedback, using a questionnaire or face-to-face interviews.

What to audit	How to audit
Information Do we gather information that matches our purpose? Is this information relevant for others? Is the information acted upon?	Review information gathered from different training interventions to determine what has been measured. Track what happens to the information gathered from a sample of training interventions.

Knowing your purpose for evaluating training is a positive step, as this will help you to work out the type of information to collect, how to do this and whom to involve. In an ideal world your purpose for evaluation would focus on outcomes and would enable you to find out about:

- the quality of the training intervention, whether in-house courses and on-the-job instruction, external provision or technology-based learning such as open learning and so on;
- the learning people gain from the training intervention;
- the way their learning changes their workplace activity;
- the effect of this learning and these changes on a wider scale, for example impact on departments, customers and the organization.

Also, in an ideal world other people would recognize their role in this process. Managers would see that they also needed to do things differently to assist in the transfer of learning to the workplace. Learners would recognize the value of measuring what they had learned as part of the transfer of learning into their daily routines. The time spent on evaluation would be seen as worthwhile and in itself a process to learn from.

As this is not an ideal world, you may find yourself alone in seeing the relevance of evaluating training. Your purpose may be more political, for example to build support for the training function, to keep a programme alive or to keep your job! Your purpose will influence the type of information you gather, what actions you take as a result and how you present the findings.

Other people may not see the relevance of the process to them and show no interest either in becoming involved or in the information you can provide to them. If a learner's manager is not engaged in the process, then it may be more difficult for them to gain the most from their experiences.

These are some of the potential barriers that might stop you reaching the ideal. To overcome these you could:

- find out the interests of those who should be involved in evaluation and ask them about the type of information they would want;
- show the benefits of measuring the outputs of training to ensure that resource and effort are applied appropriately;

- find other organizations where managers are successfully involved in evaluation and use these as case studies to support your ideas.

Evaluation strategy

Do you have a plan for putting your evaluation in place? Think about the following issues:

What to audit	*How to audit*
Strategy Do we agree what we want to measure before any training intervention, whether one-off courses or long-term programmes? Do we agree the roles of people to be involved? Do we have methods for collecting information about the current situation to compare with what happens after training? Do we set timescales for monitoring outcomes? Do we agree contingency plans if findings show that expected learning is not happening? Do we agree how our findings will be reported back?	Compare recent training interventions to find out what evaluation was carried out, how this was agreed and who was involved. Compare recent training interventions and list how much and what type of involvement managers had. Review the methods you use to set a benchmark of how things are before the training. Review the methods you use to monitor progress, how you identify triggers for corrective actions and how effective this is. Track what happens to the information gathered from a sample of training interventions.
Range of measurements Does our strategy encompass: ● processes for training needs analysis? ● training design, the methods and content? ● training delivery? ● learning outcomes? ● impact of change on the organization?	Compare recent training interventions to build up a step-by-step description of the processes gone through, from deciding that training was needed to measuring results and impact. Review information gathered from different training interventions to determine what has been measured as well as aspects that have not.
Resources Do we account for evaluation activities when organizing training so that there is sufficient resource for this?	Review the percentage of training time and costs allocated to evaluation activities to determine if this is sufficient to achieve what is intended.

Deciding to evaluate training means that you are undertaking activities that add value to the training itself:

- Learning can be activated through the process of evaluation and transferred to the workplace.
- People's level of awareness of the benefits of training can be raised to increase support for training.

It is worth all the effort to feel convinced that the training people are involved in is what they need and that their managers know what they have to do to apply this learning in the workplace. The systematic training cycle and the evaluation of training should run together as a series of complementary activities to ensure that training brings about real learning and changes everyday practice:

> It was a real pleasure to work with the organization that appointed first line managers and trained them before they took up their new posts. The company identified their training needs and asked us to design a series of half-day workshops based on leadership, communication and so on. We invited the senior managers to an overview of what we intended to include in the training so that they could change the content to meet their needs and work out what they would have to do differently to manage these people. Also, we agreed how the training would be evaluated. This was to be a combination of practical activities during the training to gauge the learning taking place and on-the-job observation and coaching by the senior managers over the first three months. We met the learners after one month to hear more about their perceptions of what they had learned and what this meant to their everyday routine, and combined this with the senior managers' feedback on the impact on their departments.
>
> Together we had created a model for training and evaluation which does not leave evaluation as the last thing you do but sees it as relevant to all phases of training:

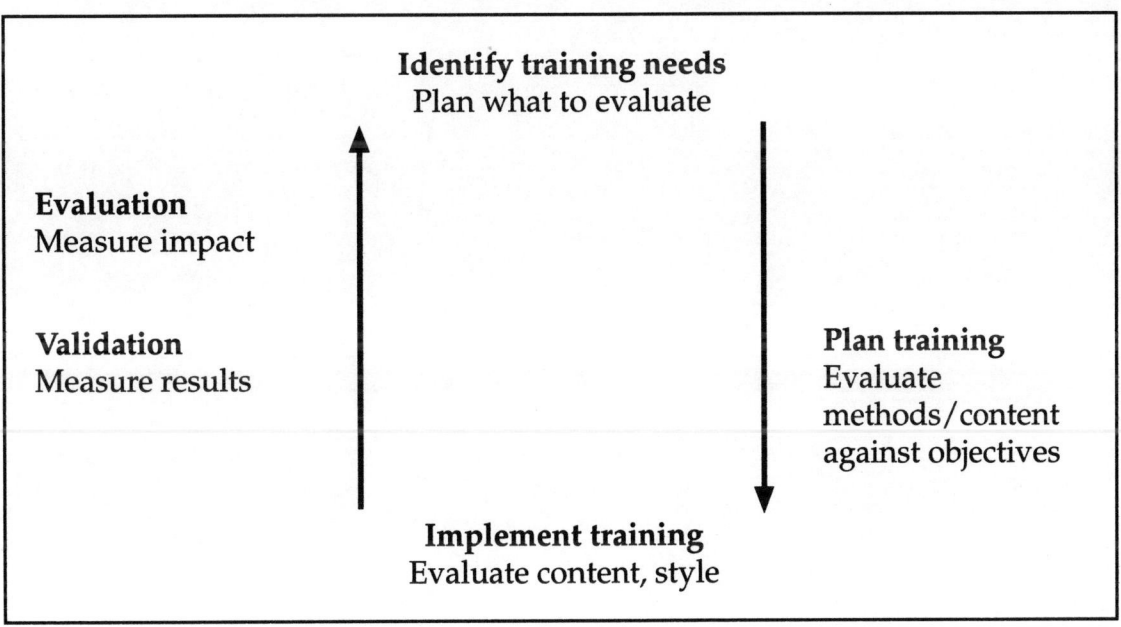

To win support for creating a strategy you could try:

- making any proposed plans straightforward and easy to implement;
- ensuring that all evaluation feedback and findings are reported fairly to encourage trust in the process.

3

Audit action plan

The Audit action plan will help you with your evaluation audit. It provides an outline for recording your findings and actions. It also serves as a reminder to check the progress of your actions to make sure that they have the effect you anticipate.

As you begin your audit it will be worth considering:

- whom you need to ask for backing for this task;
- how you intend to win this backing;
- whom you can ask for help in this task;
- where you can find information;
- what timescale you will allow for completing the task;
- how you intend to involve other interested parties such as managers;
- what methods you will use to report your findings.

Your audit can be a useful way to start a dialogue with other people to encourage their involvement in training and the evaluation of the results.

Audit action plan

This form will help you to record what you have audited, your findings and the actions you and others intend to take in the future. Monitor your progress in turning your plan into practice.

WHAT TO AUDIT	SUMMARY OF AUDIT FINDINGS	PROPOSED ACTIONS by whom & timescales	PROGRESS REVIEW – ACTIONS IN PLACE AT:			
			1 month	3 months	6 months	12 months
1 Organizational culture: ● Forward planning ● Communicating information ● Feedback						
2 The value of training: ● Making training count ● Training provision						
3 Readiness for learning ● Identifying training needs ● Learning						
4 Purpose of evaluating training ● Purpose ● Focus ● Involvement ● Information						

WHAT TO AUDIT	SUMMARY OF AUDIT FINDINGS	PROPOSED ACTIONS by whom & timescales	PROGRESS REVIEW – ACTIONS IN PLACE AT:			
			1 month	3 months	6 months	12 months
5 Evaluation strategy ● Strategy ● Range of measurements ● Resources						

AUDIT CHECK: Are your actions making a difference? Make notes about the impact of your actions on training and evaluation:

PART TWO

The instruments

Introduction

The instruments are organized in two groups:

- **A Measuring results**
  There are 18 instruments, with ready-to-use materials, to help you to measure the extent of people's learning – both what they have actually achieved and their perceptions. The section begins with an introduction that explains what is involved in measuring results, the methods used in the instruments and the format the instruments are written in. There is an index for easy reference and a checklist to help to keep a record of the instruments you plan to use.

- **B Measuring impact**
  There are six instruments, illustrating six techniques for gathering information. Each instrument contains ready-to-use materials to help you measure the difference that the learning makes in the workplace. Again the section begins with an introduction explaining what measuring impact involves, describing the methods and format of the instruments and how the techniques for gathering information can be adapted for different situations. There is an index for easy reference and a checklist to help to keep a record of the instruments you plan to use.

To get the best from the instruments, it is worth spending time to ensure that the people involved, whether learners, their managers or other interested parties, are motivated and committed to taking part in the evaluation.

Make notes about what you will discuss and agree this when you brief people, using the following points as a guide. You can also make notes of what actually happens at the briefings so that you can deal with unresolved issues.

Briefing points to agree	Briefing notes	Briefing outcome
● The proposed training intervention ● Your and their expectations about the training ● The purpose of the evaluation ● The strategy for evaluation ● Their role in the evaluation ● The benefits to them from the evaluation		

Once you have won the support of those involved, you are ready to find the instrument or set of instruments that will meet your needs. You may be able to use them as they are presented or you may find it best to adapt them to meet your specific needs. The intention is that the instruments provide a sound basis to start measuring results and impact in a way that makes the evaluation of training an integral part of the learning process.

Use the grid entitled Planning evaluation each time you are involved in measuring results and impact. This will help you with the implementation of the instruments. Record the combination of instruments you want, the method you intend to use, how much time these will need before, during and after training, and who will be involved.

Planning evaluation

Training intervention:

Planned instruments	Method of use	Time required			Who is involved		
		Before training	During training	After training	Before training	During training	After training
Measuring results:							

Planned instruments	Method of use	Time required			Who is involved		
		Before training	During training	After training	Before training	During training	After training
Measuring impact:							

A

Measuring results

Introduction

To measure results you need a clear picture of where people are now and where they are aiming for in terms of their knowledge, understanding, and technical and behavioural skills:

| KNOWLEDGE, UNDERSTANDING AND SKILLS BEFORE TRAINING | *compared to* | EXPECTED KNOWLEDGE, UNDERSTANDING AND SKILLS AFTER TRAINING |

Before going further, it may be worth checking that your methods for creating these pictures are working; that you and others do share a common understanding of what the training is setting out to achieve.

Once your background work has been done, measuring results will help you to see if people have made that journey or at least gone some way towards it:

| KNOWLEDGE, UNDERSTANDING AND SKILLS BEFORE TRAINING | ? ? ? ? ? ? ? ? ? ? ? ? | EXPECTED KNOWLEDGE, UNDERSTANDING AND SKILLS AFTER TRAINING |

To establish what has been achieved, you are looking for answers to the following questions:

- Did we train the right people appropriately?
- Were the methods we selected the most appropriate?
- Did we design the best content to meet our objectives?
- Was the training delivered in an effective way?
- To what extent have people learned from the training?
- Do people's perceptions about the training support the results?

To help you find the answers, you can try out instruments that deal with the following topics:

- Training needs analysis
- Training methods
- Training design
- Trainer style
- Learning.

A variety of techniques is applied in the instruments, such as:

- Questionnaires and rating scales
- Outcome assessments
- Practical assessment
- Post-it Notes and flipcharts
- Presentations
- Interviews.

You will find ready-to-use materials, presented consistently to provide:

- a clear description, so that you can form an assessment of the instrument's suitability for your needs;
- an indication of when to use the instrument;
- a list of the materials you will need;
- a comparison of methods for implementation, where appropriate;
- directions for getting the best from the instrument;
- suggestions for consolidation, to help you get the most from the information you gather, including further actions to take and reporting outcomes.

The index that follows provides a quick way to find the number and title of each instrument, together with the subject areas it relates to.

Index of instruments

Key: ■ main subject area □ supporting subject area

Instrument no.	Instrument title	Page no.	Training needs analysis	Training methods	Training design	Trainer style	Learning
1	Training needs analysis	35	■				□
2	The training needs process	39	■				□
3	Training methods	43		■			
4	Training design	47			■		
5	Learner feedback	51		■	■		□
6	Interest and involvement	59		■	■		□
7	Coaching	63				■	
8	Instructing	67				■	

Index of instruments *Concluded*

Instrument no.	Instrument title	Page no.	Training needs analysis	Training methods	Training design	Trainer style	Learning
9	Trainer style	71				■	
10	Trainer profile – self-assessment	75				■	
11	Trainer profile – learner assessment	81				■	
12	Outcome assessment	87		□	□	□	■
13	Practical assessment	95		□	□	□	■
14	Learner self-assessment	101		□	□	□	■
15	Learner reactions	107		□	□	□	■
16	What have you learned?	109		□	□	□	■
17	Presenting group learning	113		□	□	□	■
18	Learning summary	115		□	□	□	■

Checklist

For each new training situation make sure you can answer YES to the following questions. If you answer NO to any, then record actions to take to make the answer YES.

Checklist questions	Yes (✓)	No (✗)	What still has to be done
1 Is there a sponsor for the training?			
2 Have specific training needs been identified?			
3 Is there an agreement about what learning will be achieved?			
4 Are managers clear about their role in the learning process?			
5 Have learners, managers and others been briefed about the value of evaluation?			
6 Is there an agreement as to what will be measured?			
7 Do you know what information is needed before the training?			
8 Is there an agreement about who will be told the outcomes of the evaluation?			
9 Are people clear about what they will do with this information?			

Now, read through the instruments and select those that will be most appropriate to help you find out what you want to know. Refer back to the grid entitled Planning evaluation on pages 27–28 to record your selections and to help you plan your methods and timings for your training.

1

Training needs analysis

Description

This instrument offers you and others the opportunity to reflect on how the training needs have been identified, how these link to the business, and the effectiveness of the analysis process in generating useful information to ensure involvement of the right people. It works for one-off training events and longer programmes.

You are asked to consider a series of questions about how the training came about in the first place, and the contribution to the training made by the process of training needs analysis. There is an opportunity for you to record your comments and the consolidation guides you towards future actions and reporting of your findings.

The instrument has a number of uses. It can help to persuade senior managers that taking time to identify training needs will ensure that investment in the development of people is directed at the right initiatives – those which have relevance to the business. This can be achieved by involving them in reviewing current training or, in retrospect, to influence a future event. Also it can help you to monitor the effectiveness of needs analysis techniques so that they can be refined and amended for future training plans.

Timing

This instrument would be appropriate:

- at the end of the training needs analysis phase so that any problems could be resolved before the actual training;
- at the end of the training to review outcomes;
- before a future training needs analysis exercise.

Materials

Sufficient copies of Document 1.1: Training needs analysis – trainer's perceptions.

Methods

Method description	Pros	Cons
Work on your own	Speeds up process	You may not have all the facts
Work with training sponsor and/or managers affected by the training	Involves other managers in training	Time-consuming to arrange

Directions
1. Select your method for working with the instrument.
2. If you are working on your own, go through the questions on Document 1.1 and record your comments.
3. If you are working with others, arrange a meeting with them, give each person a copy of Document 1.1 and ask them to record their comments in time for the meeting. At the meeting encourage a discussion about the training and the role of the training needs analysis by asking individuals for their comments.

Consolidation
1. Draw together the findings from the completed documents. Look for themes; for example, the relationship of the training to business needs and whether you are able to say 'Yes' to the questions about the effects of the analysis.
2. Identify future actions either to continue the success of your training needs analysis process or to improve on what has happened. Do this by using the questions as a checklist of factors for making training needs effective. In other words, you want to be able to describe the fit between the training and company plans. There should be a sponsor. There should be a planned approach that wins support, confirms a need, identifies gaps, identifies the right people to train, defines learning objectives and an appropriate training method as well as motivating people to learn.
3. Present this information in a format appropriate to your circumstances, for example as a short report, or as a presentation.

Training needs analysis – trainer's perceptions   Document 1.1

Take stock of the process that led to the training and record your responses to each question.

Questions	Responses
What part of company plans did the training set out to fulfil? What was the specific business objective for the training? Who sponsored the training? What methods were used to gather the information? Who was involved in the process?	

In the light of your responses, consider the following:

Did the TNA:	Yes	No	Comments
Win the support of the right people for the process?			
Confirm a training need?			
Identify gaps in knowledge and understanding?			
Identify gaps in skills?			
Identify the right people with these needs?			
Define the training/learning objectives?			
Make the methods for training clear?			
Motivate those involved to want to learn?			

Reproduced from *Evaluating Training*, Sharon Bartram and Brenda Gibson, Gower, Aldershot

2

The training needs process

Description

This instrument complements Instrument 1 as it gathers the learners' impressions of the way their training needs were identified and their expectations of the training. It works both for one-off and longer programmes. The instrument poses a number of questions for the learners to answer which relate to their involvement in the training before it has happened. They respond by selecting one of three answers to each question and there is an opportunity for them to give further information about how they think the process of identifying their training needs could have been more effective.

There are a number of uses for this instrument. You can gather information that supports you in your efforts to change how training needs are identified as well as gauging how the process prepares the learners for the training. It can also provide the means of involving others in setting expectations for training.

Timing

This instrument would be appropriate:

- at the end of the training needs analysis phase, to solve any problems before the training takes place;
- after the training, as a follow-up mechanism to establish the impact of this factor on the results achieved.

Materials

Sufficient copies of Document 2.1: Training needs analysis – learner's perceptions.

Methods

Method description	Pros	Cons
Questionnaire via internal mailing systems	Easy to administer	Low response rate Cannot check for understanding Cannot gather supporting information
One-to-one interviews	Opportunity to check understanding Opportunity to gather supporting evidence	Time to set up and carry out

Directions
1. Select your method for working with the instrument.
2. If you are using the instrument as a questionnaire, arrange for each learner to receive a copy of Document 2.1 and set a date for completion and return.
3. If you are using the instrument in one-to-one interviews, arrange meeting times with each learner. At the interview you can either ask the person to fill in Document 2.1 or use the questions as a basis for discussion.

Consolidation
1. Analyse the information you have gathered by adding up how many people have responded 'Yes', 'No' or 'Partly' to each question.
2. Identify those questions to which the majority of respondents have answered 'No' or 'Partly', and decide actions that you and others can take to improve the situation either before the training or before the next time you undertake to identify training needs.
3. Present this information in a format appropriate to your circumstances, for example as a short report, or as a presentation.

Training needs analysis – learner's perceptions *Document 2.1*

To help us continually improve our training provision, please take a few moments to reflect on how your training needs were identified. We need to know that we are matching the right people to the right training.

Proposed training: _____

Planned date: _____

Do you:	Yes	No	Partly
Know why you will be attending the training?			
Know about the content of the training?			
Feel you were involved in identifying your current knowledge, understanding and skills in the aspects to be covered by the training?			
Know how taking part in the training will help you to do your job?			
Have sufficient information about the training to be able to decide which parts will be most relevant to you?			
Know what to expect from the training, what you will learn from it and how you will apply this learning to your everyday routine?			
Know what your manager expects of you as a result of taking part in the training?			

Reproduced from *Evaluating Training*, Sharon Bartram and Brenda Gibson, Gower, Aldershot

Document 2.1 Concluded

Do you:	Yes	No	Partly
Think the training will be appropriate for you?			

Is there any other information that could have made the process of identifying your training needs more effective?

Reproduced from *Evaluating Training*, Sharon Bartram and Brenda Gibson, Gower, Aldershot

3

Training methods

Description
'Training methods' here means options like off-job training courses, open learning, on-job coaching and so on. This instrument provides a way to measure how far you, or others, have selected the right training method or combination of methods to achieve the learning objectives. It works in any training situation.

You begin by stating the aims and objectives of the training and the constraints that apply to these, and then describe your expectations against a set of variable factors that will affect the training. You move on to state the training method that you have used and describe what actually happened against the variable factors.

The main use for this instrument is to determine whether your training method was the most appropriate to meet the training aims, objectives and constraints. A secondary use is as a learning opportunity in itself for you or others.

Timing
This instrument would be appropriate:

- after the training, to establish the impact of this factor on the results achieved;
- as part of the planning phase of training, to anticipate the requirements of training so that the right method can be selected from the start.

Materials
Sufficient copies of Document 3.1: Training method.

Methods

Method description	Pros	Cons
Self-completion	Easy to do	Might be too close to the training to analyse the method objectively Deciding actions on your own is not always easy
With guidance from a mentor	Sharing of ideas, particularly in consolidation Greater opportunity to learn from the experience	Experience of mentor has to be appropriate Time to set up meetings

Directions

1. Select your method for working with the instrument.
2. Whether you are working alone or with a mentor, begin by describing the training aims, objectives and constraints.
3. Write your description in the box marked A on Document 3.1.
4. Read through the variable factors listed and use a marker pen to highlight the priority ones that relate to the training.
5. Now think about and record your expectations against these priorities in the box marked B on Document 3.1.
6. Next, describe in detail the training method you selected for the training and write this in the box marked C. You may have used one method or a combination from:

   - training course run in-house;
   - training course run in-house by external consultant;
   - external training course;
   - on-job instruction;
   - on-job coaching;
   - open learning workbook;
   - computer-based training;
   - secondment;
   - shadowing;
   - project work.

7   Complete box D by describing what actually happened against the priority variable factors.

Consolidation

1   Compare the actual outcomes to the expectations and decide:

- Has there been an acceptable match?
- What are the discrepancies?
- What additional needs exist for the learners because of the discrepancies?
- What actions would you take next time to ensure a match between expectations and outcomes?

2   Present this information in a format appropriate to your circumstances, for example as a short report, or as a presentation.

3   If presenting to others is not appropriate, you may find it worthwhile to keep a journal which may help you compile a portfolio of evidence for vocational qualifications and continuing professional development.

Document 3.1

Training method

A What learning?	B Expectations	Variable factors	D Actual	C Method
Training aims, objectives and constraints		Cost Disruption to workplace Ease of learning transfer Time for practice Networking with colleagues Group development Ease of access to learning Meeting individual learning needs Access to outside knowledge Expertise of trainer Access to technology Skills to be developed Attitudes to be changed Number of learners Company norms for learning Other:		Details of training method used

Findings: What was acceptable, where were the discrepancies, additional training needs and actions for next time

Reproduced from *Evaluating Training*, Sharon Bartram and Brenda Gibson, Gower, Aldershot

4

Training design

Description

When considering training design you are thinking, for example, about the methods you have used such as role plays and practical demonstrations together with your timings and sequence of events. This instrument helps you to take stock of all the components of your design to determine how they have affected the learning outcomes. It works with any in-house training situation.

The instrument consists of a series of statements to work through to decide whether your design matches them or whether there is action you can take in the future to increase the effectiveness of your design.

The main uses for this instrument are to enable you to improve the effectiveness of your training design and to provide a learning opportunity for others who may sometimes take the trainer's role.

Timing

This instrument would be appropriate:

- at the end of the design phase, as a means of solving potential problems with the design before training;
- after the training, to measure the effects of the design and, used in conjunction with Instruments 5 and 6, to compare learners' impressions;
- as part of a future design phase, to ensure that the right components are put together in an appropriate way.

Materials

Sufficient copies of Document 4.1: Training design.

Methods

Method description	Pros	Cons
Self-completion	Easy to do	Might be too close to the training to analyse the design objectively Deciding actions on your own is not always easy
With guidance from a mentor	Sharing of ideas, particularly at the consolidation phase Greater opportunity to learn from the experience	Experience of mentor has to be appropriate Time to set up meetings

Directions
1. Select your method for working with the instrument.
2. Whether you are working alone or with a mentor, work through the statements on Document 4.1 and decide between 'Yes', meaning your design matches the statement, and 'No', meaning your design does not match.

Consolidation
1. Go back through the statements and where you answered 'No', record actions you can take to change your training design next time.
2. Compare your personal reflections with the information obtained from the learners by using Instruments 5 and 6.
3. Present this information in a format appropriate to your circumstances, for example as a short report, or as a presentation.
4. If presenting to others is not appropriate, you may find it worthwhile to keep a journal which may help you compile a portfolio of evidence for vocational qualifications and continuing professional development.

Training design

Document 4.1

Title of training: **Date:**

To help you assess the effectiveness of your design, read through each statement and decide between YES, your design matched the statement, or NO, this aspect was not covered by your design. Place a tick (✓) in the appropriate column to indicate your assessment. If you are able to answer mainly YES, your design has more than likely been successful. Where you have answered NO, consider actions you can take next time to improve your design and make a note of these.

Design statement	YES	NO – Actions
Every aspect of the design, that is: content, methods, timings and sequence, links back to the objectives		
Methods for evaluation are designed alongside content		
There is an introduction that relates the learning to what is happening in the organization		
Activities are organized in a logical sequence for learning		
The learning is split into manageable chunks		
Activities are designed to reflect how people learn best		
There is a variety of activities to match different learning styles		
The methods used maintain learners' interest, and motivate and energize them		

Reproduced from Evaluating Training, Sharon Bartram and Brenda Gibson, Gower, Aldershot

Document 4.1 Continued

Design statement	YES	NO – Actions
The organization of activities is sympathetic to environmental factors such as time of day		
The amount of content is realistic for the time available		
Time for learners to practise is built in		
Time for feedback to learners is built in		
Time for progress checks is built in		
The language used is clear and appropriate		
All potential problems are anticipated; back-up activities, processes, materials and equipment are available		
There is a summary that draws together key learning points from the content and the learners		
Time for evaluation is built in		

5

Learner feedback

Description
This instrument provides the opportunity for learners to give their impressions about their training. It works with individuals, groups, one-off training or longer programmes. It can easily be adapted to work with external training provision. This type of activity should not be underestimated, as can happen if it is referred to as a 'happy sheet' – this fact does detract from the value of the information that can be gathered.

The instrument covers a range of aspects:

- The relevance of topics
- The effectiveness of activities
- Meeting objectives
- Lasting impressions.

The learners respond to a series of statements by marking rating scales, selecting from options and completing open-ended questions.

As far as uses are concerned, the comprehensive nature of the instrument means that you can gather helpful information about learners' impressions to compare with your own, particularly relating to training design (see Instrument 4) and, to some extent, the training delivery as well as the learning achieved. Another use for the instrument is as a means of helping the learners to reflect on their experience, to appreciate the value of what they have learnt so that they are motivated to transfer this learning into their everyday routine.

Timing
This instrument would be appropriate:

- throughout training, to give the learners sufficient time to make their judgements;
- at the end of training, to gather learners' impressions;
- after external training provision, to measure the effectiveness of the external provider.

Materials
Sufficient copies of Document 5.1: Learner feedback.

Methods

Method description	Pros	Cons
Filled in by the individual in a one-to-one training situation	Easy to organize Encourages the individual to be reflective	Value to the learner lost if not explained at the outset of the training Might respond in a way that they think you want
Filled in by each individual, if training a group	Easy to organize Encourages the individuals to be reflective	Value to the learners lost if not explained at the outset of the training Might respond in a way that they think you want
As a basis for a group discussion, if training a group	Encourages the individuals to be reflective Encourages individuals to share experiences and learn from each other	Value to the learners lost if not explained at the outset of the training Some views may not be heard Time required

Directions

1. Select your method for working with the instrument.
2. For all three methods you need to prepare Document 5.1 by:
   - filling in your training topics in the table provided under the heading 'Relevance of topics';
   - filling in your training activities in the box provided in the section headed 'Effectiveness of activities';
   - filling in your training methods in the box provided in the section headed 'Effectiveness of methods'.
3. For all three methods ensure that you allow sufficient time for the completion of this instrument and that you explain the relevance of it at the start of the training.

4 If the instrument is to be used individually or in a group, give out sufficient copies of Document 5.1 and set a time for completion. Collect the completed forms.
5 If the instrument is to be the basis for a group discussion, give out sufficient copies of Document 5.1 and work through the sections in turn, gathering views from the group. Record the majority views on to a copy of Document 5.1.

Consolidation

1 Look for patterns in the responses to help you to answer the questions:

- What has worked for the learners in the training?
- What has not worked for the learners in the training?
- What learning may have been missed as a consequence?
- What improvements have the learners suggested?

2 Decide actions you can take in the future to build on strengths and overcome weaknesses.
3 Present a summary of this information in a format appropriate to your circumstances, for example as a short report, or as a presentation.
4 If presenting to others is not appropriate, you may find it worthwhile to keep a journal which may help you compile a portfolio of evidence for vocational qualifications and continuing professional development.

Document 5.1 **Learner feedback**

Title of training: **Date:**

Relevance of topics
Read down the list of topics covered by the training and rate their relevance to you in your job by putting a mark in the appropriate column.

Topic	Very relevant	Some relevance	Not relevant

Document 5.1 Continued

Effectiveness of activities

> The activities used in the training were:

Read each statement and select the activity from the box above that you would choose to complete the statement.

The most helpful activity was:

The activity that was easiest to draw out learning points from was:

The activity that was hardest to draw out learning points from was:

Reproduced from *Evaluating Training*, Sharon Bartram and Brenda Gibson, Gower, Aldershot

Document 5.1 Continued

Effectiveness of methods

```
The methods used in the training were:
```

Read each statement and select the method from the box above that you would choose to complete the statement.

The training method that best suited me was:

```

```

The training method I had most difficulty with was:

```

```

Meeting objectives
Answer each question and provide further details to support your response.
Did the programme achieve the objectives?   Yes/No/Partly
Please explain your selection:

Did you get constructive feedback?   Yes/No/Partly
Please explain your selection:

Did you get practical ideas to try back at work?   Yes/No/Partly
Please explain your selection:

Would you change the training in any way?   Yes/No/Partly
Please explain your selection:

Reproduced from *Evaluating Training*, Sharon Bartram and Brenda Gibson, Gower, Aldershot

Document 5.1 Concluded

Lasting impressions
Complete each of the following statements:
If someone asked me about the training I would say ...

The materials from the training, for example handouts, that I would not miss are ...

The materials from the training that I would not want to give back are ...

If someone asked me what I would have missed if I had not participated in the training I would say ...

Reproduced from *Evaluating Training*, Sharon Bartram and Brenda Gibson, Gower, Aldershot

6

Interest and involvement

Description
As the title of this instrument suggests, it provides a method for gathering information from learners about their feelings during their training. It works best with in-house training courses and can easily be adapted to check other aspects, for example the ease or difficulty of applying the learning from activities to the workplace.

The learners are asked to plot on a graph their level of interest and involvement throughout the training.

This instrument introduces variety to the way information is gathered from learners. The information that is collected can be used to support findings from other instruments such as Instrument 3, Training method, and Instrument 4, Training design. This instrument can also provide additional information to the trainer who is measuring the impact of their style on the learning outcomes, for example in Instruments 9 and 10. For the learners, it is an opportunity to take responsibility for what is happening to them so that the success of the training can be constantly measured and actions taken to focus on the intended learning outcomes.

Timing
This instrument would be appropriate:

- throughout training, to give the learners an opportunity to make their judgements.

Materials
Sufficient copies of Document 6.1: Interest and involvement.

Methods

Method description	Pros	Cons
Filled in by each person as the training progresses with no additional discussion	Instant reactions to their experiences	Might need reminding to complete Might become stalled by the routine
Filled in by each person as the training progresses with additional discussion, individually or as a group	Instant reactions to their experiences Opportunity to check for understanding – own and others – and probe points	Might need reminding to complete Might become stalled by the routine May not want to disclose views in a discussion Time required

Directions

1. Before you start, check that Document 6.1 meets your requirements. For example:

   - Are you running more than four activities?
   - Would it be helpful to name the activities rather than to number them?

   If so, tailor the content of Document 6.1 to match your situation.

2. Select your method for working with the instrument.
3. For both methods, give each person a copy of Document 6.1 at the start of the training and explain what you want them to do.
4. If there is to be no discussion, collect the completed graphs at the end of the training.
5. If there is to be a discussion, ensure that there is time in the training to accommodate this and ask individuals or groups:

   - What have been the high spots for them as reflected in their graph?
   - What made these high spots?
   - What have been the low spots for them as reflected in their graph?
   - What made these low spots?

6. Make notes on a copy of Document 6.1 and collect the completed graphs.

Consolidation

1. Look for patterns in the responses to help you to answer the questions:
   - What has worked for the learners in the training?
   - What has not worked for the learners in the training?
   - What learning may have been missed as a consequence?
   - What improvements have the learners suggested?

2. Decide actions you can take in the future to build on strengths and overcome weaknesses.
3. Present a summary of this information in a format appropriate to your circumstances, for example as a short report, or as a presentation.
4. If presenting to others is not appropriate, you may find it worthwhile to keep a journal which may help you compile a portfolio of evidence for vocational qualifications and continuing professional development.

Document 6.1 **Interest and involvement**

As your training progresses, use the graph below to plot your level of interest and involvement by marking with a cross (✘). At the end of the training join the crosses with a line to create a profile of how involved and interested you have been in your learning.

Title of training: **Date:**

Level of interest and involvement: HIGH to LOW across Introduction, Activity 1, Activity 2, Activity 3, Activity 4, Summary

Please add comments to help to explain your choices:

62

Reproduced from *Evaluating Training*, Sharon Bartram and Brenda Gibson, Gower, Aldershot

7
Coaching

Description
This instrument gives you and others the opportunity to assess how you have applied the skills of coaching when working with individuals.

A set of task skills and a set of process skills are listed and you are asked the question: Did you use these skills? Your responses will help you to determine your effectiveness as a coach.

The instrument has two main uses. First, it will help you to measure the impact of your coaching style on the learning outcomes. Second, it provides a means for self-development; answering the question will encourage you to find ways to improve your personal skills.

Timing
This instrument would be appropriate:

- at the end of a coaching session, to assess how you have applied your coaching skills;
- after subsequent coaching sessions, to monitor your progress.

Materials
Sufficient copies of Document 7.1: How are my coaching skills?

Methods

Method description	Pros	Cons
Self-completion	Easy to do	Can be over-judgemental about self Deciding actions on your own is not always easy

Method description	Pros	Cons
With guidance from a mentor	Sharing of ideas, particularly when consolidating learning. Greater opportunity to learn from the experience	Experience of mentor has to be appropriate. Time to set up meetings

Directions
1. Select your method for working with the instrument.
2. Whether you are working alone or with a mentor, read through the task and process skills listed on Document 7.1 and decide if you have used these skills.
3. Select from 'Yes', 'No' or 'Partly' to respond and think about actual instances during the coaching to support your answers.

Consolidation
1. Decide your future actions by looking through your answers to identify those skills that you have not used or used only partly.
2. Consider what effect the skill described has on the process of coaching as a whole and what you need to do next time to include this in your own approach.
3. Record your future actions on Document 7.1 and refer to this after subsequent coaching sessions to monitor your progress.
4. Present your results if appropriate to your situation.
5. If presenting to others is not appropriate, you may find it worthwhile to keep a journal which may help you compile a portfolio of evidence for vocational qualifications and continuing professional development.

How are my coaching skills?

Document 7.1

Think of the coaching session you have just run and read through the skills for coaching. Place a tick (✓) in the appropriate column to indicate how you rate yourself as a coach.

Date of session:	Did you use these skills?		
SKILLS FOR COACHING	Yes	No	Partly
Task skills			
Identifying learning needs and style			
Agreeing objectives with learners			
Assessing possible courses of action			
Agreeing courses of action			
Setting timescales for reviewing progress			
Identifying factors which inhibit learning			
Assisting the learner to apply their learning			
Process skills			
Putting the learner at ease, creating rapport			
Listening actively to the learner			
Using questions to encourage the learner to find their own solution			

65

Reproduced from *Evaluating Training*, Sharon Bartram and Brenda Gibson, Gower, Aldershot

Document 7.1 Concluded

Date of session:	Did you use these skills?		
SKILLS FOR COACHING	Yes	No	Partly
Giving feedback which encourages the learner to take actions to improve what they do			
Giving encouragement to motivate the learner			
Encouraging the learner to recognize their own achievement			

Reflect on your self-assessment and record actions you can take in the future:

Future actions:

Reproduced from *Evaluating Training*, Sharon Bartram and Brenda Gibson, Gower, Aldershot

8
Instructing

Description
This instrument gives you and others the opportunity to assess how you have applied the skills of instructing when training individuals.

A set of task skills and a set of process skills are listed and you are asked the question: Did you use these skills? Your responses will help you to determine your effectiveness as an instructor.

The instrument has two main uses. First, it will help you to measure the impact of your instructing style on the learning outcomes. Second, it provides a means for self-development; answering the question will encourage you to find ways to improve your personal skills.

Timing
This instrument would be appropriate:

- at the end of one-to-one instruction, as a means to assess how you have applied your instructing skills;
- after subsequent one-to-one instruction, to assess your progress.

Materials
Sufficient copies of Document 8.1: How are my instructing skills?

Methods

Method description	*Pros*	*Cons*
Self-completion	Easy to do	Can be over-judgemental about self Deciding actions on your own is not always easy

Method description	Pros	Cons
With guidance from a mentor	Sharing of ideas, particularly when consolidating learning Greater opportunity to learn from the experience	Experience of mentor has to be appropriate Time to set up meetings

Directions
1. Select your method for working with the instrument.
2. Whether you are working alone or with a mentor, read through the task and process skills listed on Document 8.1 and decide if you have used these skills.
3. Select from 'Yes', 'No' or 'Partly' to respond and think about actual instances during the one-to-one instruction to support your answers.

Consolidation
1. Decide your future actions by looking through your answers to identify those skills that you have not used or used only partly.
2. Consider what effect the skill described has on the process of instructing as a whole and what you need to do next time to include this in your own approach.
3. Record your future actions on Document 8.1 and refer to this after subsequent one-to-one instruction sessions to monitor your progress.
4. Present your results if appropriate to your situation.
5. If presenting to others is not appropriate, you may find it worthwhile to keep a journal which may help you compile a portfolio of evidence for vocational qualifications and continuing professional development.

How are my instructing skills?

Document 8.1

Think of the instruction you have just given and read through the skills for instructing. Place a tick (✓) in the appropriate column to indicate how you rate yourself as an instructor.

Date and subject:	Did you use these skills?		
SKILLS FOR INSTRUCTING	Yes	No	Partly
Task skills			
Agreeing objectives with learners			
Checking the previous knowledge of learners			
Introducing what has to be learned in a logical sequence			
Demonstrating what has to be learned when appropriate			
Checking learning against stages in training			
Testing learning against objectives			
Correcting errors made by learners			
Process skills			
Putting the learner at ease, creating rapport			

Reproduced from *Evaluating Training*, Sharon Bartram and Brenda Gibson, Gower, Aldershot

Document 8.1 Concluded

Date and subject:	Did you use these skills?		
SKILLS FOR INSTRUCTING	Yes	No	Partly
Listening actively to the learner			
Asking questions to engage learners in working out what to do			
Asking questions to test knowledge and understanding			
Giving information in a clear and precise way			
Giving feedback which encourages the learner to take actions to improve			
Giving encouragement to motivate the learner			

Reflect on your self-assessment and record actions you can take in the future:

Future actions:

Reproduced from *Evaluating Training*, Sharon Bartram and Brenda Gibson, Gower, Aldershot

9
Trainer style

Description
This instrument gives you and others the opportunity to reflect on your style to measure the impact of this factor on the learning outcomes. It works with one-to-one and group training and can be applied to a single training event or as a review of several.

You start by thinking of different situations in the training that stand out in your mind. You are guided through how to analyse these situations by a series of prompts and questions, leading you eventually to identifying actions to take in the future.

The main use for this instrument is as a self-development tool. By analysing your style from your experiences, you will be able to make changes to what you do to ensure that you contribute to the achievement of learning outcomes. You may find that Instrument 6 can provide supporting information if dealing with one training event.

Timing
This instrument would be appropriate:

- after training, as a mechanism for self-reflection;
- after training, as a means to monitor progress towards implementing actions.

Materials
Sufficient copies of Document 9.1: Style – situation analysis.

Methods

Method description	Pros	Cons
Self-completion	Easy to do	Can be over-judgemental about self Deciding actions on your own is not always easy
With guidance from a mentor	Sharing of ideas, particularly when consolidating learning Greater opportunity to learn from the experience	Experience of mentor has to be appropriate Time to set up meetings

Directions

1. Select your method for working with the instrument.
2. For both methods start by thinking of two or three situations which arose during the training. Choose different types of situations that stand out in your mind, such as:

   - one when you were pleased with the way you handled it;
   - one when you thought you could do better in the way you handled it;
   - one when something took you by surprise or was unexpected.

3. Describe each situation as fully as you can, using Document 9.1 to help you. Use a separate sheet for each situation. Make notes and write about:

   - what triggered the situation;
   - who was involved and your relationship with them;
   - at what point in the training the situation arose;
   - what you did/said – think of specific actions and phrases;
   - what others did/said – think of specific actions and phrases;
   - what emotions/feelings were expressed by you/others;
   - what the outcome/resolution was.

Consolidation

1. Compare your situations to see if there are any patterns, for example:

   - Are there similarities in the triggers that set off the situations?
   - Are your reactions similar across the different situations?
   - Are your reactions appropriate to the different situations?
   - Are the situations resolved satisfactorily for you and others?

2. Summarize your learning points from analysing each situation.
3. Decide future actions you intend to take to build on strengths and overcome weaknesses.
4. Present your findings if appropriate.
5. If presenting to others is not appropriate, you may find it worthwhile to keep a journal which may help you compile a portfolio of evidence for vocational qualifications and continuing professional development.

Document 9.1 — **Style – situation analysis**

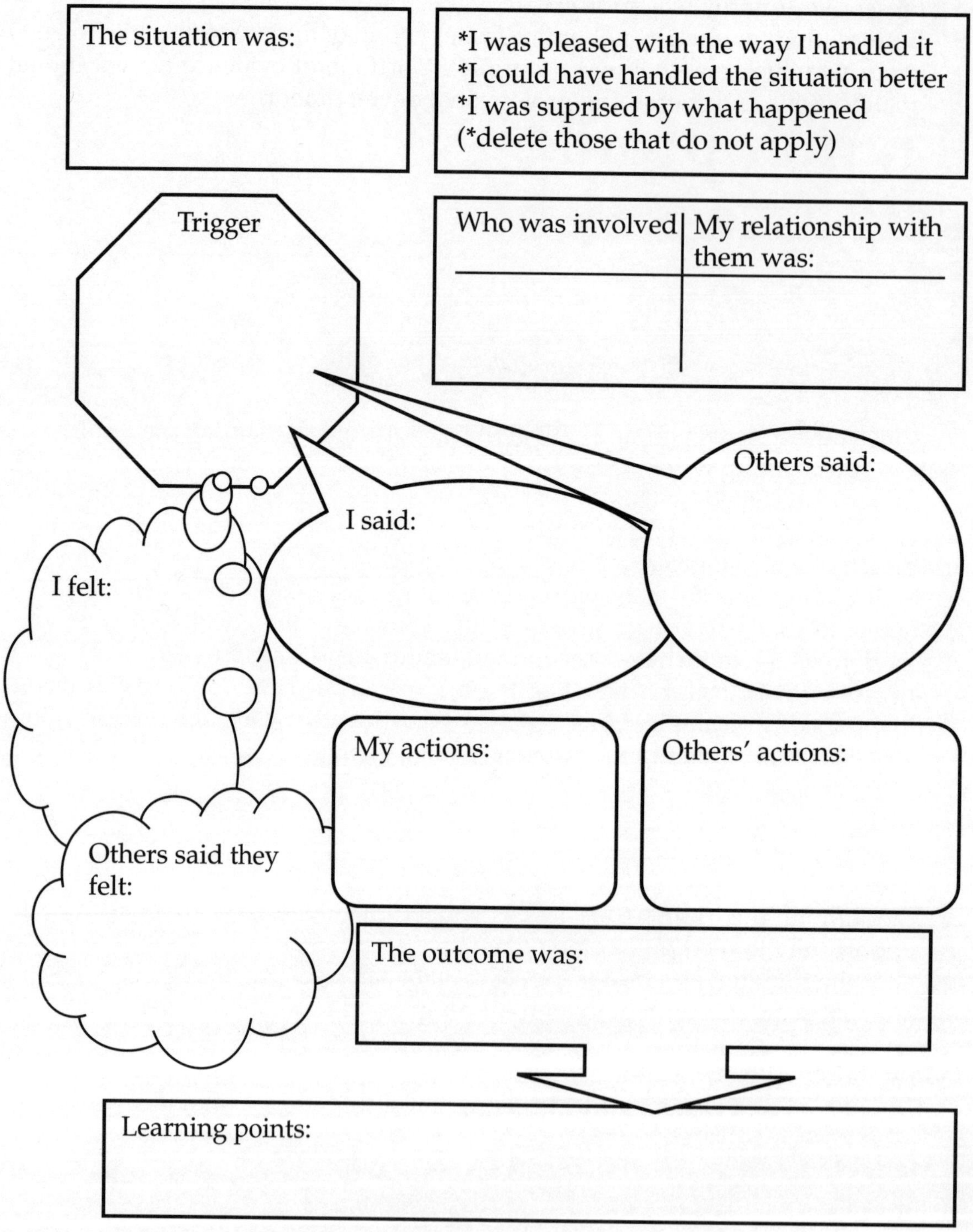

- The situation was:
- *I was pleased with the way I handled it
- *I could have handled the situation better
- *I was suprised by what happened
- (*delete those that do not apply)

Trigger

Who was involved	My relationship with them was:

I felt:

I said:

Others said:

Others said they felt:

My actions:

Others' actions:

The outcome was:

Learning points:

74

Reproduced from *Evaluating Training*, Sharon Bartram and Brenda Gibson, Gower, Aldershot

10

Trainer profile – self-assessment

Description
This instrument gives you and others the opportunity to assess your facilitation skills when working with groups.

You are presented with a range of behaviours appropriate for facilitating groups and you are invited to select from a rating scale to show how you have used each one in the group training being measured. There is also space for you to record comments to make your rating more meaningful. The instrument is designed so that you can create a profile to indicate the effectiveness of your facilitation, which in turn enables you to identify areas for future action.

This instrument has a number of uses. You can measure the impact of your facilitation skills on the learning outcomes and identify your personal development needs. If Instrument 11 is also applied, you will get a balanced view.

Timing
This instrument would be appropriate:

- throughout the training, if this is longer than one day, to give you the opportunity to record your judgements;
- after the training, as a means to reflect on behaviours;
- after subsequent training, to monitor progress in putting actions in place.

Materials
Sufficient copies of Document 10.1: Trainer profile – self-assessment.

Methods

Method description	Pros	Cons
Self-completion	Easy to do More prepared to disclose shortcomings to self	Can be over-judgemental about self Deciding actions on your own is not always easy
With guidance from a mentor	Sharing of ideas, particularly when consolidating learning Greater opportunity to learn from the experience	Experience of mentor has to be appropriate Time to set up meetings

Directions

1. Select your method for working with the instrument.
2. For both methods, work through the behaviours listed on Document 10.1 and for the training you are measuring decide a rating for how you have used the behaviours. Follow the directions on the document to indicate your rating.
3. Add comments that explain your rating, for example incidents that happened, what you said and did, what others said and did.
4. When you have worked down the whole list you will have a personal profile which reflects how you have used the behaviours.

Consolidation

1. Look back over your profile to identify:

   - behaviours that you have used effectively, that is, any rating of 4 or 5;
   - behaviours that you have used adequately, that is, any rating of 3;
   - behaviours that you need to work on, that is, any rating of 1 or 2.

2. Consider the effects of how you have used the behaviours on the learning outcomes:

   - Have you helped or hindered the learning process?
   - What learning may have been missed as a consequence?

3. Record actions you could take in the future to ensure that you are effectively using the behaviours for facilitating groups. There is space on Document 10.1 for this.

4 Present your findings if appropriate to your circumstances.
5 If presenting to others is not appropriate, you may find it worthwhile to keep a journal which may help you compile a portfolio of evidence for vocational qualifications and continuing professional development.

Document 10.1 **Trainer profile – self-assessment**

The following list describes behaviours used by trainers when facilitating groups. Think back over the training you have just facilitated and for each of the behaviours, place a dot (●) in the appropriate column to show your rating of how you have used these behaviours. Record comments that support your ratings. Once you have completed your ratings, join the dots to create your trainer profile.

Title of training:

	poor				excellent	
TRAINER BEHAVIOURS	1	2	3	4	5	SUPPORTING COMMENTS
Creates a safe environment for learning						
Agrees objectives						
Manages time						
Keeps people on track						
Sticks to the point						
Observes behaviours						
Reacts to group dynamics						
Organizes groups						
Gives information						
Gives instructions						
Maintains interest						
Uses knowledge of subject matter effectively						
Develops trust						
Empathizes with learners						
Listens						
Asks questions						

Reproduced from *Evaluating Training*, Sharon Bartram and Brenda Gibson, Gower, Aldershot

Document 10.1 Concluded

TRAINER BEHAVIOURS	poor				excellent	SUPPORTING COMMENTS
	1	2	3	4	5	
Gives feedback						
Draws people in						
Deals with problems and conflict						
Motivates people						
Energizes the group						
Other:						

Future Actions

Reproduced from *Evaluating Training*, Sharon Bartram and Brenda Gibson, Gower, Aldershot

11

Trainer profile – learner assessment

Description
This instrument complements Instrument 10 as it asks the same questions about the trainer's group facilitation skills but this time gathers the learners' impressions. The learners are given the list of facilitation behaviours and they reflect over the training to give a rating to their trainer. This in turn produces a profile that indicates where the trainer has used behaviours effectively or adequately, together with aspects that need to be worked on.

The main use for this instrument is to gain another perspective on how effective you and others are at facilitating groups and thus balance your own view of yourself. A secondary application is to give the learners experience in recognizing and assessing behaviours; this may be a useful skill to them in other aspects of their jobs.

Timing
This instrument would be appropriate:

- at the end of the training, as a means for the learners to reflect on what the trainer has done.

Materials
Sufficient copies of Document 11.1: Trainer profile – learner assessment.

Methods

Method description	Pros	Cons
Completed individually by group members	More candid response	May answer in the way they think you want Time for completion Lack of awareness of facilitation processes
Completed collectively by small groups	Sharing ideas will help with clarifying understanding Less threatening to give a group view	May answer in the way they think you want Time for completion Not all views heard Lack of awareness of facilitation processes

Directions

1. Select your method for working with the instrument.
2. For both methods, ensure that there is sufficient time in the training for this activity and explain at the start why you would like the group to provide you with this feedback.
3. If the group completes the instrument individually, give each person a copy of Document 11.1 to fill in. Stress the importance of including supporting information such as specific examples of what the trainer did. Be on hand to clarify any points. Then collect the completed profiles.
4. If the group completes the instrument collectively, organize them into small groups and give out copies of Document 11.1. Allow time for the groups to reach their collective ratings, stressing the importance of including supporting information such as specific examples of what you, the trainer, did and be on hand to clarify any points. Then ask each group to record their ratings and comments on one copy of the sheet and collect the completed profile from each small group.

Consolidation

1. Analyse the profiles by looking for patterns such as a consensus about:

   - the behaviours you have used effectively, that is, any rating of 4 or 5;
   - the behaviours you have used adequately, that is, any rating of 3;
   - areas you need to work on, that is, any rating of 1 or 2.

2 Look at your own profile and identify areas where you and the learners agree and consider:

- What are the consequences on the learning outcomes?

3 Look at your own profile and identify areas where you and the learners disagree and consider:

- How might the difference in views have happened?
- What are the consequences for the learning outcomes?

4 Present your findings if this is appropriate to your circumstances.
5 If presenting to others is not appropriate, you may find it worthwhile to keep a journal which may help you to compile a portfolio of evidence for vocational qualifications and continuing professional development.

Document 11.1   **Trainer profile – learner assessment**

The following list describes behaviours used by trainers when facilitating groups. Think back over the training you have just participated in and for each of the behaviours, place a dot (●) in the appropriate column to show your rating of your trainer. Record comments that support your ratings. Once you have completed your ratings, join the dots to create a profile of your trainer.

Title of training:

	poor				excellent	
TRAINER BEHAVIOURS	1	2	3	4	5	SUPPORTING COMMENTS
Creates a safe environment for learning						
Agrees objectives						
Manages time						
Keeps people on track						
Sticks to the point						
Observes behaviours						
Reacts to group dynamics						
Organizes groups						
Gives information						
Gives instructions						
Maintains interest						
Uses knowledge of subject matter effectively						
Develops trust						
Empathizes with learners						
Listens						
Asks questions						
Gives feedback						

Reproduced from *Evaluating Training*, Sharon Bartram and Brenda Gibson, Gower, Aldershot

Document 11.1 Concluded

TRAINER BEHAVIOURS	poor				excellent	SUPPORTING COMMENTS
	1	2	3	4	5	
Draws people in						
Deals with problems and conflict						
Motivates people						
Energizes the group						
Other:						

Reproduced from *Evaluating Training*, Sharon Bartram and Brenda Gibson, Gower, Aldershot

12

Outcome assessment

Description

This instrument enables you and others to assess the ability of learners to carry out tasks where the outcome, rather than the process used to achieve the result, is important. It is suitable for any training where there is no set sequence of actions and the finished product can be measured against standards. It works with individuals and groups on in-house training. To use the instrument for external training specific to your organization, you would need to make your standards known to the provider and agree these as a means of setting learning objectives.

The learners are asked to complete the task they have been training for and you assess the result against a pre-prepared set of components and standards. You answer the question: 'Is the standard fully met?' against each component. This instrument has a number of uses:

- Managers can involve themselves in setting the components and standards before the training.
- Knowing what has to be measured from the outset means that appropriate training methods can be selected and the training can be designed to ensure that the right learning is achieved.
- The actual learning achieved is highlighted by the assessment and, where there are deviations, you, the learner and others can decide actions to overcome the shortfall.
- The results of the assessment give you and others the opportunity to review the quality of your training method selection, training design and training style to assess how much these have contributed to the success or shortfalls of the training.
- Defining the components and standards you want learners to achieve would be a means of selecting external training, for example where your people attend public courses. Your selection would be based on how closely the objectives of the public course met your specific requirements.

Timing

This instrument would be appropriate:

- at the end of training, to assess learning achieved;
- after training, to reinforce learning;
- after external training, to test for the learning achieved, which in turn provides a guide to the effectiveness of the external provider.

Materials
Sufficient copies of Document 12.1: Outcome assessment.
Sufficient copies of Document 12.2: Outcome assessment – illustrations.

Methods

Method description	*Pros*	*Cons*
Task completed by each learner in the training environment	Easier to control in terms of timing Suits tasks that do not have to be completed in a specific place No disruption to workplace	Not all tasks suitable for carrying out in the training environment because of resource requirements
Task completed by each learner in the workplace	More realistic Suits tasks that have to be completed in a specific place	Harder to control in terms of timing, disruption to workplace

Directions
1. Before the training, work with the managers to define the components and standards for the task or tasks to be trained.
2. Together complete Document 12.1 by specifying the learning objective and breaking this down into components, and the standards to be achieved for each component. You may also find it helpful to agree what would be classed as a deviation, for future reference.
3. The two illustrations on Document 12.2 are provided as examples of the type of things you might write. They are intended as guidelines only and may not contain all of the components and standards for the tasks described.
4. Select your method for working with the instrument.
5. With either method, ensure that there are sufficient resources for the learners to complete the task.
6. If you are working with one learner, have ready the prepared Document 12.1 and ask the learner to complete the task. Assess their results against each component and standards and decide if the standards are fully met or not.

Tick the appropriate column on Document 12.1 and record any specific deviations from the standards. Give positive feedback where the standards are fully met. Give feedback about any deviations from the standards and ask questions to probe if the learner understands why they have not met the standard. Let the learner have a copy of the completed assessment sheet and agree actions to overcome the shortfalls, where necessary.

7 If you are working with a group of learners, make sure you allocate sufficient time to allow each one to complete the task and have ready a copy of the prepared Document 12.1 for each person. Ask the learners to complete the task and follow step 6 as above.

Consolidation

1 For an individual learner, review the completed Document 12.1 and pick out any aspect where the standards have not been fully met and consider:

- Was the training method right?
- Was the training design appropriate?
- Was the training style appropriate?

2 For groups of learners, look for patterns in their completed assessments to answer:

- What parts of the training have worked?
- What parts of the training have not worked?

3 Present a summary of your findings to include:

- Assessment results – the standards fully met and the deviations
- Actions agreed with learners to overcome shortfalls from standards
- Impact of training methods, design and style on the outcomes.

4 Use a presentation method that is appropriate to your circumstances, for example a short report or a presentation.

Document 12.1 **Outcome assessment**

LEARNING OBJECTIVE:				
Component	Standard	Is standard fully met?		Deviation
		YES	NO	

Reproduced from *Evaluating Training*, Sharon Bartram and Brenda Gibson, Gower, Aldershot

Outcome assessment – illustrations

Document 12.2

Illustration 1

LEARNING OBJECTIVE: Display unpackaged, loose tomatoes on fresh food section					
Component	Standard	Is standard fully met?		Deviation
		YES	NO	
Quality of product	No damaged fruit No over-ripe fruit			
Range of ripeness	A mix of ready to eat and still ripening			
Fullness of display	Full to specified limits			
Point of sale information	Information located in the right place, visible and describing correct price, country or origin, type of tomato and serving suggestions			

Document 12.2 Continued

Illustration 2

LEARNING OBJECTIVE: Write a letter that requests payment of an outstanding invoice				
Component	Standard	Is standard fully met?		Deviation
		YES	NO	
Layout	Typeface in company style Company letterhead Evenly spaced Address of recipient positioned for window envelope			
Reference details	Address of recipient correct Postcode included Correct date Your reference/our reference included Letter given a subject title			
Salutations	Name of recipient used Opens with Dear (*name*) Closes with Yours sincerely			
Content	Introduction states reason for letter Next paragraph asks for payment by a specified date Closing paragraph states further action if payment is not received			

Reproduced from *Evaluating Training*, Sharon Bartram and Brenda Gibson, Gower, Aldershot

Document 12.2 Concluded

Component	Standard	Is standard fully met?		Deviation
		YES	NO	
Writing style	Clear and precise language used Sentences of mixed length Punctuation used appropriately Grammatically correct No spelling mistakes			

Reproduced from *Evaluating Training*, Sharon Bartram and Brenda Gibson, Gower, Aldershot

13

Practical assessment

Description

This instrument enables you and others to assess the ability of learners to carry out tasks where the process of achieving the result is as important as the outcome. It is suitable for any training where there is a set of actions that contribute to the end result. It works with individuals and groups on in-house training. To use the instrument for external training specific for your organization, you would need to make your requirements known to the provider and agree these as a means of setting learning objectives.

The learners are asked to complete the task they have been trained in and you observe the skills they use and test their understanding against a pre-prepared checklist. You want to see if they use all the skills appropriately and whether they can explain what they are doing.

This instrument has a number of uses:

- Managers can become involved in setting the checklist for skills and understanding before the training.
- Knowing what has to be measured from the outset means that appropriate training methods can be selected and the training can be designed to ensure that the right learning is achieved.
- The actual learning achieved is highlighted by the assessment and you, the learner and others can decide actions to remedy any shortfall.
- The results of the assessment give you and others the opportunity to review the quality of your training method selection, training design and training style so that you can assess how much these have contributed to the success or otherwise of the training.
- Compiling a checklist of skills you want learners to demonstrate and specifying the supporting understanding they need would be a means of selecting external training, for example where your people attend public courses. Your selection would be based on how closely the objectives of the public course met your specific requirements.

Timing
This instrument would be appropriate:

- at the end of training, to assess learning achieved;
- after training, to reinforce learning;
- after external training, to test for the learning achieved, which in turn provides a guide to the effectiveness of the external provider.

Materials
Sufficient copies of Document 13.1: Practical assessment.
Sufficient copies of Document 13.2: Practical assessment – illustration 1.
Sufficient copies of Document 13.3: Practical assessment – illustration 2.

Methods

Method description	*Pros*	*Cons*
Task completed by each learner in the training environment	Easier to control in terms of timing Suits tasks that do not have to be completed in a specific place No disruption to workplace	Not all tasks suitable for carrying out in the training environment because of resource requirements
Task completed by each learner in the workplace	More realistic Suits tasks that have to be completed in a specific place	Harder to control in terms of timing, disruption to workplace

Directions
1. Before the training, work with the managers to compile the checklist of skills and specify underlying knowledge relevant to the task or tasks to be trained.
2. Together complete Document 13.1 by specifying the task and the learning objectives and describing the skills demonstration you will ask the learner to complete. Develop a checklist of:

   - What to look for – observable skills
   - What to ask – questions to check understanding.

3. The example on Document 13.2 shows the type of checklist you might develop for a manual skill. The example on Document 13.3 shows the type of checklist you might develop for a behavioural skill. These illustrations are

intended as guidelines only and may not represent a full checklist for the tasks described.

4 Select your method for working with the instrument.
5 For either method, ensure that there are sufficient resources for the learners to complete the task.
6 If you are working with one learner, have ready the prepared Document 13.1 and ask the learner to perform the demonstration.

- Assess their performance; have they used the expected skills and if so, have these been applied effectively?
- Ask the set of questions to check their understanding.
- Record the results of the skills demonstration in the space provided on Document 13.1.
- Give positive feedback where the learner has performed effectively.
- Give feedback about any learning gaps and ask questions to probe if the learner understands why they have not achieved the expected learning.
- Agree actions to overcome the learning gaps, where necessary, recording these on the assessment sheet, and give a copy of the completed assessment to the learner.

7 If you are working with a group of learners, make sure you allocate sufficient time to allow each individual to complete the skills demonstration and have ready a copy of the prepared Document 13.1 for each person. Begin the first demonstration and follow step 6 as above until the entire group has received a completed assessment.

Consolidation

1 For an individual learner, review the completed assessment sheet and note any aspect where there is a learning gap and consider:

- Was the training method right?
- Was the training design appropriate?
- Was the training style appropriate?

2 For groups of learners, look for patterns in their completed assessment sheets to answer.

- What parts of the training have worked?
- What parts of the training have not worked?

3 Present a summary of your findings to include:

- Assessment results – the skills learned and supporting understanding gained
- Actions agreed with learners to overcome learning gaps
- Impact of training methods, design and style on the outcomes.

4 Use a presentation method that is appropriate to your circumstances, for example as a short report or as a presentation.

Document 13.1

Practical assessment

Name: Job title:	LEARNING OBJECTIVES:		
TASK:		Results	Actions
DESCRIPTION OF SKILLS DEMONSTRATION	What to ask – questions to check		
What to look for – observable skills understanding			

98

Reproduced from *Evaluating Training*, Sharon Bartram and Brenda Gibson, Gower, Aldershot

Practical assessment – illustration 1

Document 13.2

Name: *Chris Chow* Job title: *Checkout operator*				
	TASK: *Key entering a barcode*			
	LEARNING OBJECTIVES: *Key enter barcodes for items that you are unable to scan*			
	DESCRIPTION OF SKILLS DEMONSTRATION	*Ask operator to scan a basket of shopping which includes two large items which are the same.*		
		What to ask – questions to check understanding *How do you know that a product has not scanned?* *What would you do if you had two of the same items that wouldn't scan?* *What would you do if none of the items scanned?*	**Results**	
		What to look for – observable skills *Recognising when a product has not scanned* • *No green light* • *No sound (beep)* • *Last item scanned still on P.O.D. (point of display)* *For unscanned item:* • *Press star button on keyboard* • *Key in all numbers* • *Press enter on keyboard* • *Check P.O.D. to make sure amount has registered* *Dealing with more than one of same item:* • *Press star button on keyboard* • *Key in all numbers* • *Press quantity button and select number key* • *Press enter on keyboard* • *Check P.O.D. to make sure amount has registered*		**Actions**

Reproduced from *Evaluating Training*, Sharon Bartram and Brenda Gibson, Gower, Aldershot

Document 13.3 **Practical assessment – illustration 2**

Name: *Jo Soap*
Job title: *Trainee manager*

TASK: *Recruitment interview*

LEARNING OBJECTIVES: *Assess a candidate for selection*

DESCRIPTION OF SKILLS DEMONSTRATION
1. *Learner to carry out role play at end of training.*
2. *Learner to carry out an actual selection interview.*

What to look for – observable skills	What to ask – questions to check understanding
• Creates rapport • Sets the agenda for the interview • Uses fair selection criteria • Asks open questions • Asks questions that are relevant • Probes responses to clarify meaning • Gathers evidence from candidates to match the selection criteria • Uses appropriate body language • Manages time • States what will happen next to finalize the interview	*How did you define your selection criteria?* *How do you ensure that your selection criteria are fair?* *What is a fair selection criterion and how does this differ from an unfair one?* *What signs would you be looking for that might suggest a candidate is being frank and open?* *What is sometimes called the 'Halo effect' and how would you avoid this?* *What are some of the pitfalls when interviewing and how would you overcome them?*

Results

Actions

Reproduced from *Evaluating Training*, Sharon Bartram and Brenda Gibson, Gower, Aldershot

14

Learner self-assessment

Description
This instrument gives the learners the opportunity to assess their level of learning from the training. It works with in-house training whether on a one-to-one basis or in group training. It is relevant for one-off events or longer-term training.

Each learner selects from a rating scale to indicate what they think is their level of learning in relation to the knowledge and understanding the training intends to help them to develop, as well as the technical and behavioural skills. They also have the opportunity to record what help they need from the trainer.

The instrument has a number of uses:

- To establish the learners' perceptions of their progress, which can be compared to results from outcome assessments (see Instrument 12) and practical assessments (see Instrument 13).
- To enable the trainer to clarify the specific learning expected from the training.

Timing
This instrument would be appropriate:

- at relevant stages in the training, such as after key exercises, at the mid-point and so on to assess levels of learning;
- at the end of the training, to assess levels of learning.

Materials
Sufficient copies of Document 14.1: Self-assessment.
Sufficient copies of Document 14.2: Self-assessment summary chart.

Methods

Method description	Pros	Cons
Completed by learners, with no follow-up discussion, in one-to-one or group situations	Quick to complete	No opportunity to check understanding
Completed by learners, with a follow-up discussion, in one-to-one or group situations	Opportunity to check understanding and clarify points Opportunity to reinforce learning points	Time required for training

Directions

1 Select your method for working with the instrument.
2 For both methods prepare Document 14.1 by writing in the specific knowledge and understanding the training should have helped the learners to acquire at the point they complete the instrument. Do the same for the technical and/or behavioural skills.
3 Explain to the learners the usefulness to them of completing the instrument and how you will be able to add your feedback from outcome assessments and/or practical assessments to confirm the learning that is taking place.
4 Give the learners a copy of the prepared Document 14.1 and, if there is to be no discussion, ask them to complete it and hand it back to you.
5 If there is to be a discussion, ensure that there is time in the training to accommodate it. Give the learners a copy of the prepared Document 14.1 and ask them to complete it and, before they hand it back, ask:

- Are there some aspects that have been learned fully and what would they say to support this?
- Are there some aspects that have been learned partially and what would they say to support this?
- Are there some aspects where more help is needed and what would they say to support this?

Make notes of the responses and collect the completed assessments.

Consolidation

1 If you are using this instrument at a stage in the training, you can concentrate on those aspects on which the learners want more help and plan remedial actions to bring you back on target for achieving the learning outcomes.

2   If you are using this instrument at the end of the training, you should take into account supporting evidence from any outcome assessments or practical assessments undertaken by the learners about which they have had your feedback. This is important as it may alter the ratings for an individual.
3   Look for those aspects where the training did not lead to the expected level of learning and review:

   - appropriateness of training method;
   - appropriateness of training design;
   - the information from the learners about the additional help they need.

4   Decide actions to ensure that this learning is achieved and agree this with others. For example, it might be that further practice in the workplace is the solution and so involve the learners' managers, for example, in carrying out further outcome assessments.
5   When you use this instrument with groups you may find it helpful to transfer the results on to Document 14.2: Self-assessment summary chart.
6   Present your findings in a format appropriate to your circumstances, for example as a short report or as a presentation.

Document 14.1 **Self-assessment**

Listed below are the knowledge and understanding, along with the behavioural or technical skills, this training will help you to acquire.

Learning objective:			
Knowledge and understanding you should be able to demonstrate:	Learned fully	Learned partially	More help please
Technical or behavioural skills you should be able to demonstrate:			

Actions the trainer could take to help me would be:

Reproduced from *Evaluating Training*, Sharon Bartram and Brenda Gibson, Gower, Aldershot

Self-assessment summary chart

Document 14.2

Learning objective:

Key: X = learned fully
\ = learned partially
Left blank = needs more help

Names

Expected knowledge and understanding

Expected technical or behavioural skills

Reproduced from *Evaluating Training*, Sharon Bartram and Brenda Gibson, Gower, Aldershot

15

Learner reactions

Description
This instrument is fun to complete and provides a quick and easy alternative to traditional 'happy sheets' given out at the end of training. It is adaptable to work with individual learners as well as groups on in-house training. It is relevant for one-off and longer-term training.

You decide the feedback you want from the learners and present this as a series of questions, usually on flipcharts. The learners make their response directly on to the flipcharts.

The main use for this instrument is to gather information about the learners' impressions of particular aspects of the training as chosen by the trainer.

Timing
This instrument would be appropriate:

- at the end of training, as a means to encourage feedback from learners.

Materials
Flipchart sheets.
Sufficient supply of Post-it Notes.

Methods

Method description	Pros	Cons
Completed by individual learners or groups of learners	Raises awareness of learning Opportunity to reflect on experience	May respond in a way that is seen as expected

Directions

1. Have ready three or four flipcharts, each headed with a different question you want to ask the learners. Your options for questions are limitless; you need to work out in advance what it is you want feedback on. Some examples are:

   - What have you learned that you expected to learn?
   - What have you learned that you did not expect?
   - What have you enjoyed the most?
   - What would you change about the training?
   - What has helped you the most?
   - What would you have liked to spend more time on?
   - What are your lasting impressions of the training?
   - What would you tell others about the training?
   - What differences will this training make to you in your job?

2. Ask the learners to respond to the questions. To speed up this process you could give them a set of Post-it Notes to write their responses on, one per Post-it, and then attach these to the relevant flipchart. Alternatively you could tell the learners to write their responses directly on to the flipcharts.
3. In a group situation, give the learners time to read everyone else's responses; then sum up their experience of the training.
4. With an individual, ask them to reflect on their responses and sum up their experience of the training.

Consolidation

1. Look for themes in the responses to help you to identify:

   - the elements of the training that have worked for the learners;
   - the elements of the training that have not worked for the learners;
   - the learning that may have been missed as a consequence;
   - the learning that has been achieved, both the expected and unexpected;
   - suggestions from the learners for making improvements that you will try out next time.

2. Review your training process in the light of these findings, for example:

   - Had the right training needs been identified?
   - Was the training method appropriate?
   - Was the training design appropriate?

3. Sum up your learning from this analysis.
4. Decide actions that may be necessary to ensure that all expected learning is achieved.
5. Present your findings in a way that is appropriate to your circumstances, for example as a short report or as a presentation.
6. If presenting to others is not appropriate, you may find it worthwhile to keep a journal which may help you compile a portfolio of evidence for vocational qualifications and continuing professional development.

16

What have you learned?

Description

This instrument provides a quick, easy and energizing way for learners to reflect on their learning. It is adaptable to work with individuals and groups on in-house and external training. It is relevant for one-off events and longer-term training.

The learners are issued with Post-it Notes and asked to write statements about what they have learned. These statements are then displayed and discussed. There is plenty of guidance to help the learners draw out their learning from their experiences during the training.

The instrument has numerous uses:

- It gathers information about the learners' impressions of their own learning, as well as helping to make them aware of what has changed for them as a result of the training. Not only will this process highlight expected learning, but it will provide information about learning that the trainer may not be aware of.
- When the instrument is used with groups, the sharing of ideas can increase awareness of what learning has taken place. Whether used with an individual or a group, the instrument can be a motivating factor in encouraging the transfer of learning into everyday routines.
- Working with an instrument like this one alongside outcome assessments (see Instrument 12) and practical assessments (see Instrument 13) can provide the learners and trainers with a balanced view of what learning outcomes have been achieved.
- The instrument can also be used to debrief learners when the training has been done by somebody else, for example after external training.

Timing

This instrument would be appropriate:

- at the end of training, to summarize what learning has taken place from the learners' perspective;

- after external training, to establish what learning has taken place from the learners' perspective. This can help to measure the effectiveness of the external provider.

Materials
Sufficient copies of Document 16.1: What have you learned?
Sufficient Post-it Notes.
A means for displaying the Post-it Notes, for example a flipchart or wall space.

Methods

Method description	Pros	Cons
Completed by individual learners or groups of learners	Raises awareness of learning Shows range of learning	May respond in a way that is seen as expected

Directions
1. Give the learners a supply of Post-it Notes. Alternatives to these are cards or pieces of paper. If you use these alternatives ensure that there is some space where they can be spread out once completed by the learners.
2. Issue copies of Document 16.1, which explains the steps to follow. Check for understanding.
3. Encourage the learners to post up their statements of learning. Ask for clarification of any statement that seems unclear.
4. With an individual learner or a group, help them to identify themes and to organize their statements according to these themes.
5. Make notes of the statements that show that the expected learning outcomes have been achieved.
6. Make notes of the statements that show that unexpected learning has taken place.
7. Encourage the learners to retrieve their Post-it Notes to keep as feedback to themselves about the training.

Consolidation
1. From your notes, summarize what expected learning has taken place.
2. Decide actions that need to be taken if there are still gaps in the learning achieved.
3. From your notes, summarize what unexpected learning has taken place and the potential benefits of this to the individual.
4. Present your findings in a way that is appropriate to your circumstances, for example as a short report or as a presentation.

What have you learned?

Document 16.1

You have been given a supply of Post-it Notes; on each one write a statement that describes something that you have learned through the training you have just been involved in.

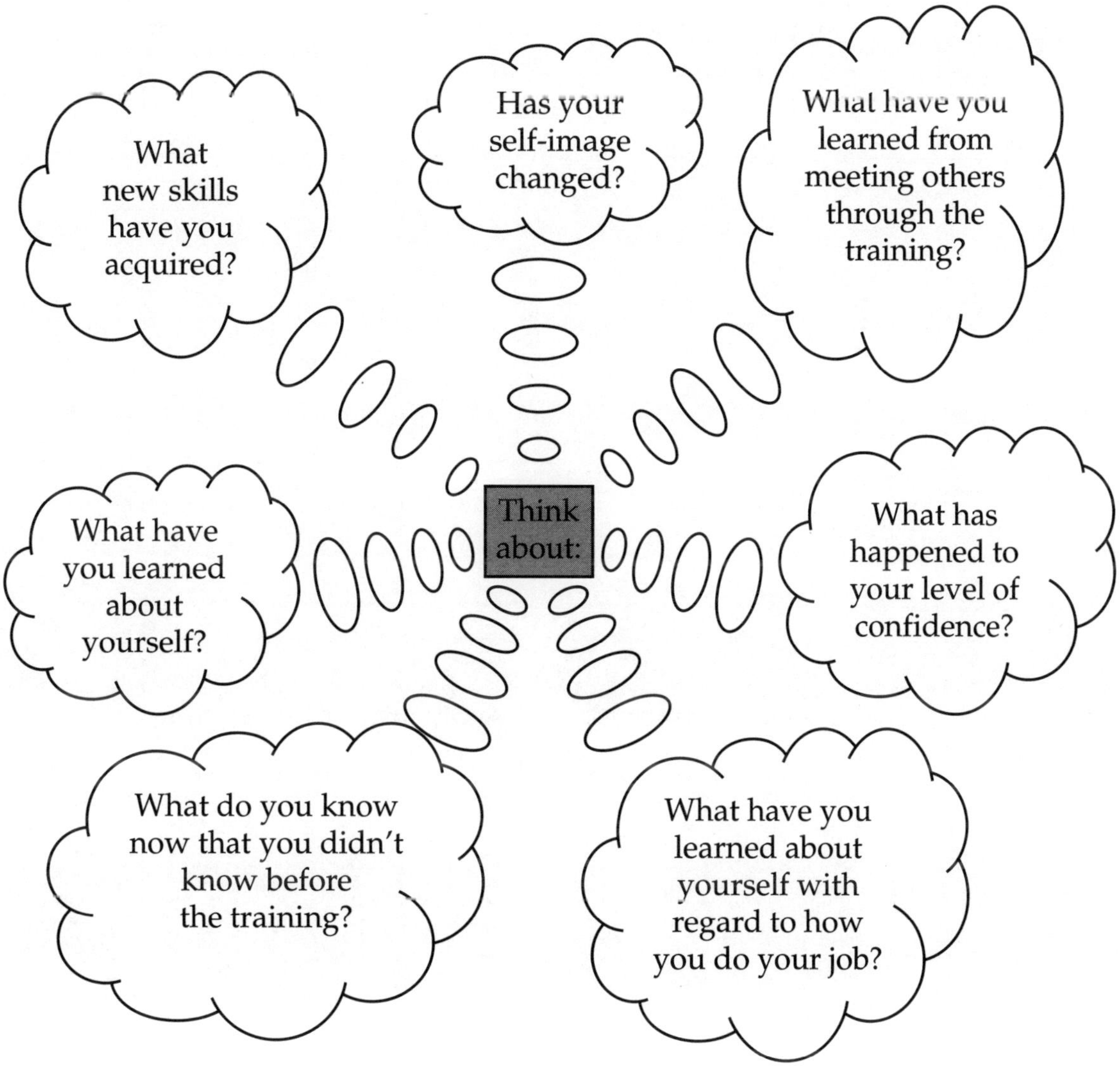

Think about:

- What new skills have you acquired?
- Has your self-image changed?
- What have you learned from meeting others through the training?
- What have you learned about yourself?
- What has happened to your level of confidence?
- What do you know now that you didn't know before the training?
- What have you learned about yourself with regard to how you do your job?

Write as many Post-it Notes as you want.

111

Reproduced from *Evaluating Training*, Sharon Bartram and Brenda Gibson, Gower, Aldershot

17

Presenting group learning

Description
This instrument generates feedback from learners about the expected and unexpected learning that has taken place. It is most suitable with in-house behavioural skills training and is a creative and entertaining way to work with groups. It is applicable for one-off as well as longer-term training.

The learners are asked to make a presentation about what they have learned. The style of the presentation is left open, although they are given ideas to make their presentations unique.

The main uses of the instrument are to gather information about the learners' impressions of their own learning as well as to help to make them aware of what has changed for them as a result of the training. The sharing of ideas can increase awareness of what learning has taken place, which in turn can be a motivating factor to encourage the transfer of learning into everyday routines.

Timing
This instrument would be appropriate:

- at selected times over longer-term training, to measure progress of learning;
- at the end of training, to summarize what has been learned.

Materials
There are no specific materials required for this instrument, although it may be useful to have available flipcharts, artistic props or other presentation technologies.

Methods

Method description	*Pros*	*Cons*
Presentations by small groups	Sharing ideas can help to reinforce learning Opportunity to clarify misunderstandings Identifies gaps in learning Individuals get encouragement from working in a small group.	Time needed for the training Amount of information generated may not be easy to analyse Individuals' learning issues not highlighted

Directions

1. Divide the group into teams of three or four people.
2. Ask each team to make a presentation about what they have learned.
3. Explain that their presentation can take any style, and encourage them to be as creative as they want. Alternatively you could assign styles to the teams, for example their presentations could take the form of a:

   - newscast
   - song
   - pantomime
   - demonstration
   - sales pitch.

4. Allow preparation time and be on hand to clarify any points raised by the teams.
5. Watch each presentation in turn and make notes about the learning that the team is putting across.
6. At the end of each presentation summarize the learning points back to the team so that they can add any items you may have missed.

Consolidation

1. Review your notes from the presentations to summarize:

   - the expected learning that has taken place;
   - the unexpected learning that has taken place.

2. If you are using the instrument at selected times during longer-term training, you can decide if remedial action is required to keep the learning relevant.
3. If you are using the instrument at the end of training, you can decide actions to take in the workplace and whom to involve if there appear to be gaps in the expected learning.
4. Present your findings in a way that is appropriate to your circumstances, for example as a short report or as a presentation.

18

Learning summary

Description
This instrument adopts an interview style to encourage learners to talk about what they have learned. It works with individuals and groups on any type of training, whether one-off or longer-term, in-house or external.

The learners start by completing the phrase: 'I have attended this training and I have learned...' and are then prompted by the question, repeated several times: 'And what else have you learned?' to encourage them to probe their own learning.

The main use for this instrument is to enable the learners to clarify what they have learned, which in turn can identify gaps still to be addressed, as well as motivating the learners to apply what they have learned to their everyday routine.

Timing
This instrument would be appropriate:

- at the end of training, to establish learning outcomes;
- after attendance on external training, to establish learning outcomes and give some indication of the effectiveness of the provider.

Materials
Tape recorder and tapes.

Methods

Method description	Pros	Cons
Taped interviews with individual learners and groups of learners	Ensures all information is captured for analysis. Maintains momentum of the process	Reticence of learners about being recorded. Recording may lead to guarded responses
Interviews with individual learners and groups of learners where the trainer takes notes	Note-taking less obtrusive than tape-recording.	Points can be missed. Notes leave out details which may be important when looking back

Directions

1. Explain to the learners that the purpose of the instrument is to enable them to clarify their learning.
2. If taping the interview, reassure them that the reason for taping the interview is to ensure that information is not lost or misinterpreted, which can happen with written notes. Explain that they will receive a copy of the feedback you pick out from the tape and that the tape will be wiped clean.
3. Ensure that the learners are happy with their interview being taped. If this is not the case take notes instead.
4. When working with one learner, explain that the instrument starts by asking them to complete a statement and then uses a probing question repeatedly to help them clarify what they have learned. Begin the interview by asking the learner to complete the statement:

   - I have attended this training and I have learned ...

   Ask the learner the follow-up question:

   - And what else have you learned?

   Continue using the follow-up question until the learner has said all they can about their learning.

5. When working with a group of learners, arrange chairs so that the group sits in a circle. Explain that they must each respond to the statement:

   - I have attended this training and I have learned ...

   Listen to each person's response before moving on to the next person, and continue in this way until all the learners have said all they can about their learning.

Consolidation

1. Review the tapes or your notes to pick out themes such as:

   - what people have learned about themselves;
   - what people have learned about others;
   - how their learning will affect them in their jobs.

2. Summarize:

   - the expected learning that has taken place;
   - the unexpected learning that has taken place;
   - potential gaps in learning to be addressed.

3. Prepare a copy of your review to give as feedback to the learners.
4. Wipe any tapes clean.
5. Decide actions to take in the workplace and whom to involve in dealing with any learning shortfall.
6. Present your findings in a way that is appropriate to your circumstances, for example as a short report or as a presentation.

B

Measuring impact

Introduction
Evaluating training is more than measuring results. You and others will also want to know what difference the learning makes. There are three aspects on which to measure impact:

- The department/section where the learners work
- The organization/business in a wider sense
- The learners themselves.

To measure the impact on these three aspects you need to establish:

- indicators that describe the situation as it is before the training;
- indicators that describe the situation as it is after the training.

This adds a further dimension to the model drawn in Section A: Measuring results:

| KNOWLEDGE, UNDERSTANDING AND SKILLS BEFORE TRAINING | *compared to* | EXPECTED KNOWLEDGE, UNDERSTANDING AND SKILLS AFTER TRAINING |

| SITUATION BEFORE TRAINING | *compared to* | SITUATION AFTER TRAINING |

The instruments in this section will help you and others to gauge the difference that the learning makes. We have selected six techniques for doing this:

1 Questionnaire
2 Open-ended statements
3 Quantifiable evidence
4 Write a story
5 Draw a picture
6 Learning journal.

Not only are the instruments a source of ready-to-use materials; they also illustrate how to construct and use each technique. Our guidance notes accompanying each instrument explain how you can adapt these to work just as well with all aspects when measuring impact. This is one feature of the guidance notes. Again the material provides:

- a clear description, so that you can form an assessment of the instrument's suitability for your needs;
- an indication of when to use the instrument;
- a list of the materials you will need;
- a comparison of methods for implementation, where appropriate;
- directions for getting the best from the instrument;
- suggestions for consolidation, to help you get the most from the information you gather, including further actions to take and reporting outcomes.

The index opposite provides a quick way to find the number and title of each instrument, together with the aspect we have written it for and its suitability for adaptation to other aspects.

Index of instruments

Key: ■ written for this aspect □ can be adapted for this aspect

Instrument no.	Instrument title	Page no.	Department or section	Organization or business	Learners
19	Draw a picture	123	■	□	□
20	Quantifiable evidence	127	■	□	□
21	Write a story	133	□	■	□
22	Open-ended statements	137	□	■	□
23	Learning journal	141	□	□	■
24	Impact questionnaire	149	□	□	■

Checklist

For each new training situation make sure you can answer YES to the following questions. If you answer NO to any, then record actions to make the answer YES.

Checklist questions	Yes (✓)	No (✗) What still has to be done
1 Is there a sponsor for the training?		
2 Have specific training needs been identified?		
3 Is there an agreement about what learning will be achieved?		
4 Are managers clear about their role in the learning process?		
5 Have learners, managers and others been briefed about the value of evaluation?		
6 Is there an agreement as to what will be measured?		
7 Do you know what information is needed before the training?		
8 Is there an agreement about who will be told the outcomes of the evaluation?		
9 Are people clear about what they will do with this information?		

Now, read through the instruments and select those that will be most appropriate to help you find out what you want to know. Refer back to the grid entitled Planning evaluation on pages 27–28 to record your selections and to help you plan your methods and timings into your training.

19
Draw a picture

Description
This instrument uses a creative technique to measure the impact of learning on the department or section. It works with one-off and longer-term training for in-house and external provision.

Managers and their learners are asked to draw two pictures, one before the training to depict the current situation in relation to the proposed training. The second picture is drawn after the training and a comparison made between the two to determine the differences the training has made.

The main uses for the instrument are to put the learning achieved into the wider context of what happens in the department or section, as well as to encourage dialogue between managers and learners to ensure that potential blocks to the learning making a difference are removed. The pictures themselves are just a vehicle to help communication.

Adaptability
This technique could be used to measure the impact of learning on the organization or business, where the training in question affects people at all levels in the organization. A sample of people could be asked to create their pictures and, through discussion, these could be compared to see if there is a consistent view of where the organization is starting from. A comparison of the discussions about the second pictures would show if there was a common view of how the training was contributing to the aims of the organization or business, and this would highlight points for action.

The technique could also be adapted to measure the impact of learning on the learner by asking people to relate their drawings more specifically to their perceptions of their knowledge and skills, confidence, expertise and so on.

Timing
This instrument should be applied:

- before the training, to assess the current situation;
- at a suitable interval after the training, to identify the changes the training has brought about.

Materials
Sufficient copies of Document 19.1: Draw a picture.
Supply of A3 and flipchart paper.
Tape recorder and tapes.

Methods

Method description	*Pros*	*Cons*
Manager alone produces pictures of before and after training	Easy to administer	No involvement of learners Reticence about drawing a picture
Manager and learner(s) produce joint pictures of before and after training	Brings managers and learners together	Some views may prevail over others Some people may have to compromise on their views Reticence about drawing a picture
Manager and learner(s) produce individual pictures of before and after training as the basis for discussion	All views prevail Easier to identify differences in perceptions Brings managers and learners together	Reticence about drawing a picture

Directions
1. Select your method for working with the instrument.
2. For all three methods explain to those involved that you want to tape the discussion you have with them so that they have an accurate record of how they see the current situation. This will be invaluable when it comes to comparing their pictures after the training.

3　Check that the use of the tape is acceptable. If it appears to be causing a problem you could make detailed notes instead.
4　The process of using this instrument is the same for all three methods. Begin by providing sufficient copies of Document 19.1 and encourage those involved to produce their visual images. Make available larger sheets of paper. Either remain on hand as the pictures are completed or arrange a time for a discussion.
5　Once the pictures are complete, discuss with those taking part the meaning of their images and tape their responses.
6　Where people have produced individual drawings it is also worth highlighting the similarities and differences in how they see things, as this may have an impact on what the training can achieve. Encourage the group to agree actions to overcome potential problems that their differing views may pose for the training.
7　Keep all pictures and the taped discussion for comparison later.
8　Agree a suitable interval after the training and repeat the drawing process, providing another copy of Document 19.1 and larger sheets of paper.
9　Discuss with those involved the meaning of their second picture, replay their tape and show their first picture.
10　Invite them to remark on the differences that emerge between the two pictures and what they are saying now compared to their comments after the first drawing.

Consolidation

1　Summarize the changes the training has made to the department or section based on the drawings and discussions and consider:

- Does this represent the full extent of the changes?
- Will the effects of the changes become more apparent over time?

2　Consider whether the changes represent a fair return on the investment made in the training.
3　Present your findings in a way that is appropriate to your circumstances, for example as a short report or as a presentation.

Document 19.1 **Draw a picture**

Draw a picture that describes how you see your department/section working. The picture should relate to aspects of your work that the training is designed to improve. Ask yourself:

- What works well?
- What could be improved?
- How do others see your department?

Create whatever image you like to illustrate your thoughts. Begin by specifying your learning objective.

Learning objective:

Do not be limited by this size of paper. Use A3 or flipchart paper if you want.

Reproduced from *Evaluating Training*, Sharon Bartram and Brenda Gibson, Gower, Aldershot

20

Quantifiable evidence

Description

This instrument measures the impact of learning on the department or section. It works with one-off and longer-term training for in-house and external provision. The manager is asked to work through a list of measurable criteria and to select those relevant to his/her department or section. Actual measurements are recorded against these criteria before and after the training so that the extent of changes can be judged.

The main uses for this instrument are to help managers to identify:

- how their department or section currently works;
- where the training can make a difference

and then help them to assess:

- to what extent this happens.

Also, it can highlight for managers the type of information they should be maintaining about their operation to ensure that it functions efficiently and effectively.

Adaptability

This technique could be used to measure the impact of learning on the organization or business, where the training in question affects people at all levels in the organization. Senior managers could compile a list of measurable criteria together with current actual measures that describe the way the organization works, indicating where the training can make a difference. Comparing these values to those identified after the training would help to show how much of a difference was being achieved.

Similarly, it could be used to measure the impact of learning on the learners by asking them to compile a list of measurable criteria specific to getting their job done. Comparing the actual measures of the criteria before and after training would show how much of a difference the training was making.

Timing

This instrument should be applied:

- before the training, to assess the current situation;
- at a suitable interval after the training, to identify the changes that the training has brought about.

Materials

Sufficient copies of Document 20.1: Quantifying evidence.

Methods

Method description	*Pros*	*Cons*
Managers alone identify the measurable criteria and actual measures before and after training	Easy to administer	No involvement of learners
Managers and the learners in their department or section work together to identify the measurable criteria and actual measures before and after training	Brings managers and learners together Allows for discussion	Takes more time

Directions

1. Select your method for working with the instrument.
2. For both methods, provide those involved with Document 20.1.
3. Help them to identify the measurable criteria relevant to their department or section; invite them to add criteria of their own.
4. If they know the actual measures, ask them to complete the column headed 'Before training' on Document 20.1 and to keep this sheet for future reference.
5. Keep a copy of Document 20.1 completed to this stage for reference by you or others delivering the training.
6. If they do not know the actual measures, help them to plan what they have to do to gather the information before the training. Again, they need to keep Document 20.1 for future reference.

7 Ensure that you receive a copy of Document 20.1 completed to this stage for reference by you or others carrying out the training.
8 Agree a suitable interval after the training and repeat the process of recording actual measures, this time in the column headed 'After training' on Document 20.1.
9 Encourage those involved to summarize the difference the training has had on the measurable criteria.

Consolidation

1 Review the changes the training has made to the department or section based on the differences to the measurable criteria and consider:

- Does this represent the full extent of the changes?
- Will the effects of the changes become more apparent over time?
- Will the measurable criteria continue to change over time?

2 Consider whether the changes represent a fair return on the investment made in the training.
3 Present your findings in a way that is appropriate to your circumstances, for example as a short report or as a presentation.

Document 20.1 **Quantifying evidence**

Consider the situation before and after the training. Select only those measurable criteria relevant to the training in question and fill in the details. Start by specifying the learning objective.

Learning objective:		
Measurable criteria	**Before training**	**After training**
Time taken		
Amount completed		
Amount completed right first time		
Unit cost		
Quality of communication ● right people ● right time ● right information		
Level of complaints		
Amount of wastage		
Level of positive feedback		
Turn-around time		
Level of repeat business		
Level of new business		
Level of late completions		
Attitude to work		
Absenteeism		
Other:		

Reproduced from *Evaluating Training*, Sharon Bartram and Brenda Gibson, Gower, Aldershot

Document 20.1 Concluded

Summarize the difference the training has made, based on the measurable criteria:

Reproduced from *Evaluating Training*, Sharon Bartram and Brenda Gibson, Gower, Aldershot

21
Write a story

Description
This instrument offers a creative way to measure the impact of learning from large-scale training projects upon the organization or business. Examples might be: Investors In People initiatives, total quality programmes, change management programmes or any training which affects people at all levels in the organization.

Selected people across the organization are asked to write a story about the situation before the training and to write a second story after the training is complete. They have complete freedom to write what they want to, and a frank response is encouraged. The comparison between the two stories provides evidence of what has changed and how much of a difference the training has made.

The main uses for the instrument are to gather a range of perceptions about how the organization works before the training. This is helpful in gauging whether there is a consistently held view of the organization. Also, a comparison of perceptions after the training shows whether a consistent message is getting through, and the extent of changes and differences the training has made to the way in which the organization operates.

Adaptability
This instrument is a suitable alternative to Instrument 19: Draw a picture, to measure the impact of learning on departments/sections and learners.

Timing
This instrument should be applied:

- before the training, to assess the current situation;
- at a suitable interval after the training, to identify the changes the training has brought about.

Materials
Sufficient copies of Document 21.1: Write a story.

Methods

Method description	Pros	Cons
Selected people work together to produce collective stories	Sharing of ideas Speedy process	Some views may prevail over others Bringing the whole group together at once
Selected people work individually to produce stories and are brought together to compare their perceptions	All views prevail Participants see other people's point of view in comparison to own perceptions	Time to organize Amount of information to analyse

Directions

1. Select your method for working with the instrument.
2. If the group produces a collective story, bring them together and provide sufficient copies of Document 21.1. Give encouragement as the group members reach agreement and write their story. Once this is completed, ask the group to summarize the key points of what they have written. Then ask them to keep the story for future reference and take a copy for your own reference.
3. If the group members work individually to write their own stories, provide sufficient copies of the Document 21.1. Set a time limit for completing the stories and arrange a meeting for the group to come together to compare their writings. At the meeting allow time for the group members to read each other's stories, and ask each person to summarize the key points of what they have written. Invite the group members to remark on the similarities and differences in their stories and how this in itself will have an impact on what the training can achieve. Encourage them to agree actions to overcome potential problems that their differing views may pose for the training. Finally, take a copy of each story for future reference and ask the group to keep their copies for the same purpose.
4. For both methods, agree a suitable time interval after the training and repeat the writing process. Provide more copies of Document 21.1 if required.
5. For both methods, ask those involved to compare the second story with the first and to summarize what has changed because of the training.
6. Make notes of the summaries and take copies of the second set of stories for further analysis.

Consolidation

1. Review in detail the stories from before and after training to draw out:

    - similarities and differences;
    - the changes in perceptions of those involved;
    - where the training has made a difference;
    - what the training has had no impact on;
    - whether the full extent of the changes from training has been realized;
    - whether more differences will become apparent over time.

2. Consider whether the changes represent a fair return on the investment made in the training.
3. Present your findings in a way that is appropriate to your circumstances, for example as a short report or as a presentation.

Document 21.1 **Write a story**

In order to capture a freeze-frame description of your organization at this moment, write a story in the frame below from your point of view. You might include:

- the aims of the organization, how these are met, how these are understood;
- what works well in the organization and what could be improved;
- what you would recommend about the organization to others;
- how people do their jobs and work together;
- the image the organization displays to the outside world, including customers, suppliers and the community.

Begin with a brief description of the training project.

Training project:

Continue on separate sheet if necessary.

Reproduced from *Evaluating Training*, Sharon Bartram and Brenda Gibson, Gower, Aldershot

22

Open-ended statements

Description

This instrument provides a more structured way to measure the impact of learning on the organization or business. It works best for large-scale training projects such as Investors In People initiatives, total quality programmes, change management programmes or any training which affects people at all levels in the organization.

Selected people are given a series of open-ended statements, which they are asked to complete before and after training. The comparison between the two sets of responses provides evidence of what has changed and how much of a difference the training has made.

The main uses of the instrument are to gather a range of perceptions about how the organization works before the training. This is helpful in gauging whether there is a consistently held view of the organization. Also, a comparison of perceptions after the training shows whether a consistent message is getting through, and the extent of changes and differences the training has made to the way in which the organization operates.

Adaptability

This technique can be adapted to measure the impact on the department or section. Instead of broad statements, you could make them specific to the training. For example, if the programme was 'Teambuilding', you could write statements relating to this for the departments to complete.

The technique can also be adapted to measure the impact on the learner. Again, instead of broad statements you could write some that were specific for the individual. For example, if the learner has been on Customer Service training, the statements would be about that subject.

Timing
This instrument should be applied:

- before the training, to assess the current situation;
- at a suitable interval after the training, to identify the changes that the training has brought about.

Materials
Sufficient copies of Document 22.1: Open-ended statements.

Methods

Method description	Pros	Cons
Selected people collectively complete the statements	Sharing of ideas Speedy process	Some views may prevail over others Bringing the whole group together at once
Selected people work individually to complete the statements and are brought together to compare their perceptions	All views prevail Participants see other people's point of view in comparison to own perceptions	Time to organize Amount of information to analyse

Directions
1. Select your method for working with the instrument.
2. If the group completes the statements collectively, bring them together and provide sufficient copies of Document 22.1. Give encouragement as the group members reach agreement on what to write to complete the statements. Once this is done, ask the group to summarize the key points of their responses, and to keep the statements for future reference. Take a copy for your own reference.
3. If the group members work individually to complete the statements, provide sufficient copies of Document 22.1. Set a time limit for completing the statements and arrange a meeting for the group to come together to compare their responses. At the meeting allow time for the group members to read each other's statements, and invite them to remark on the similarities and differences in their responses and how this in itself will have an impact on what the training can achieve. Encourage the group to agree actions to overcome potential problems that their differing views may pose for the training.

Finally, take a copy of each set of completed statements for future reference and ask the group to keep their copies for the same purpose.
4 For both methods, agree a suitable time interval after the training and repeat the process of completing statements. Provide everyone with another copy of Document 22.1.
5 For both methods, ask those involved to compare their second set of responses with their first and to summarize what has changed because of the training.
6 Make notes of what is said and take copies of the second set of completed statements for further analysis.

Consolidation

1 Review in detail the sets of completed statements from before and after training to draw out:

- where the training has made a difference;
- what the training has had no impact on;
- whether the full extent of the changes from training has been realized;
- whether more differences will become apparent over time.

2 Consider whether the changes represent a fair return on the investment made in the training.

3 Present your findings in a way that is appropriate to your circumstances, for example as a short report or as a presentation.

Document 22.1   **Open-ended statements**

Take a few moments to read through the following statements and then complete each one in a way that you think accurately describes what it is like in your organization.

I would describe communication here as . . .

The best way to describe peoples attitude to their work is . . .

The levels of quality we achieve are . . .

I would describe our business processes as . . .

The relationship we have with our suppliers could be described as . . .

Our reputation with our customers could be summed up as . . .

Our competitors see us as . . .

In describing our cost efficiency I would say that . . .

Our approach to innovation is . . .

In describing how we make decisions here, I would say that . . .

We reward people for . . .

Our attitude towards training is . . .

Reproduced from *Evaluating Training*, Sharon Bartram and Brenda Gibson, Gower, Aldershot

23

Learning journal

Description
This instrument provides a creative alternative to action plans and keeping diaries to measure the impact of learning on the learner. It works for longer-term training as well as training options such as open learning and self-directed study.

The learners are asked to keep a journal that reflects their thoughts before, during and after their learning. They are given guiding questions to answer, to show the type of information to record. The final stage takes the form of a summary for the learners to identify the changes and differences the training has made to them.

The main use for this instrument is to help the learners to develop the process of reflection and review so that they can gain the most from the training. Also, by keeping a journal, the learners are developing their ability to analyse situations, which will lead them to a more detailed assessment of the changes and differences they have experienced.

Adaptability
This instrument can be adapted for use jointly by learners and managers to measure the impact on the department or section of long-term training initiatives. To do this you would need to change the focus of the guiding questions away from the individual and towards issues about how the department works.

Similarly, someone in a strategic role could gather information from all areas to maintain a journal that measures the impact at an organizational level.

An option for creating the journal is to write it more traditionally as a diary, using Documents 23.2, 23.3 and 23.4 as prompts.

Timing
This instrument should be applied continuously:

- before the training, to record perceptions about the training;
- during the training, to summarize key learning points and intended actions;
- at a suitable interval after the training, to identify the changes the training has brought about.

Materials

Sufficient copies of Document 23.1: Learning journal – instructions.
Sufficient copies of Document 23.2: Learning journal – before learning.
Sufficient copies of Document 23.3: Learning journal – your journey.
Sufficient copies of Document 23.4: Learning journal – summary.

Methods

Method description	*Pros*	*Cons*
Learner or group of learners completes the journal on their own	Easy to do More prepared to be frank with self Not influenced by another person's point of view	Could miss points Motivation to maintain journal could wane
Learner or group of learners completes the journal with guidance from a mentor	Can bounce ideas off another person Greater opportunity to learn from the experience More disciplined to complete the work	Experience of mentor has to be appropriate Time to get together Could affect spontaneity of what is recorded

Directions

1 Introduce the learners to the ideas of keeping a journal, giving them sufficient copies of Document 23.1. Check for understanding.
2 Explain the methods for working with the instrument and ask the learners to select the method that best suits them.
3 Explain that they should start their journal before the training by completing Document 23.2. This helps them to clarify their expectations. Give out the document.
4 Explain that they are to record their journey during and after the training, using Document 23.3. Give out a copy of the document and ask them to make as many copies as they need for their various entries.
5 Arrange to meet the learners at a suitable interval after the training to review progress.
6 Ask them to prepare for this meeting by completing a summary using Document 23.4. Give out the document.
7 At the meeting ask them to talk you through their journal entries. Make notes of what is said.

8 Ask them to tell you about their summary of the changes and differences the training has made and either make notes or ask for a copy of Document 23.4.

Consolidation

1 Use your notes and the summary of the changes and differences to consider:
   - where the training has made a difference;
   - what the training has had no impact on;
   - whether the full extent of the changes from training has been realized;
   - whether more differences will become apparent over time;
   - whether the training methods, design and delivery have had a positive or negative influence on the outcomes for the learners.

2 Consider whether the changes represent a fair return on the investment made in the training.
3 Decide actions to take in the future to improve the selection of training methods as well as the quality of design and delivery.
4 Present your findings in a way that is appropriate to your circumstances, for example as a short report or as a presentation.

Document 23.1 **Learning journal – instructions**

To capture the ways in which your learning influences you, it would be useful to keep a journal and routinely record, for example:

- what you do differently as the result of your learning;
- how this difference shows up in your everyday routines;
- how you are meeting your targets and objectives.

Here is a suggested method of going about it:

1. Begin by describing your views about your forthcoming learning:

    - Why are you doing it?
    - What changes do you think it will make to you?
    - What are your hopes and fears?

    Write your thoughts on Document 23.2.

2. During the course of your learning, use as many copies of Document 23.3 as you need. Along the 'road' write in milestone events:

    - What happened during your learning that stood out?
    - What did it look, sound and feel like?

    Also write down things that people around you are saying that link back to how you are progressing on your learning journey. It might be useful to write these periodically, for example daily or weekly as you feel is appropriate, so that you can chart your progress.

3. At the end of your course of learning, take some time to reflect on how you have changed. Write your thoughts on Document 23.4. These might cover:

    - how you saw yourself before the learning programme;
    - how you see yourself now at the end of the programme;
    - the changes other people have noticed;
    - the differences you have made to how you do your job;
    - how you are meeting your targets and objectives.

Reproduced from *Evaluating Training*, Sharon Bartram and Brenda Gibson, Gower, Aldershot

Learning journal – before learning

Document 23.2

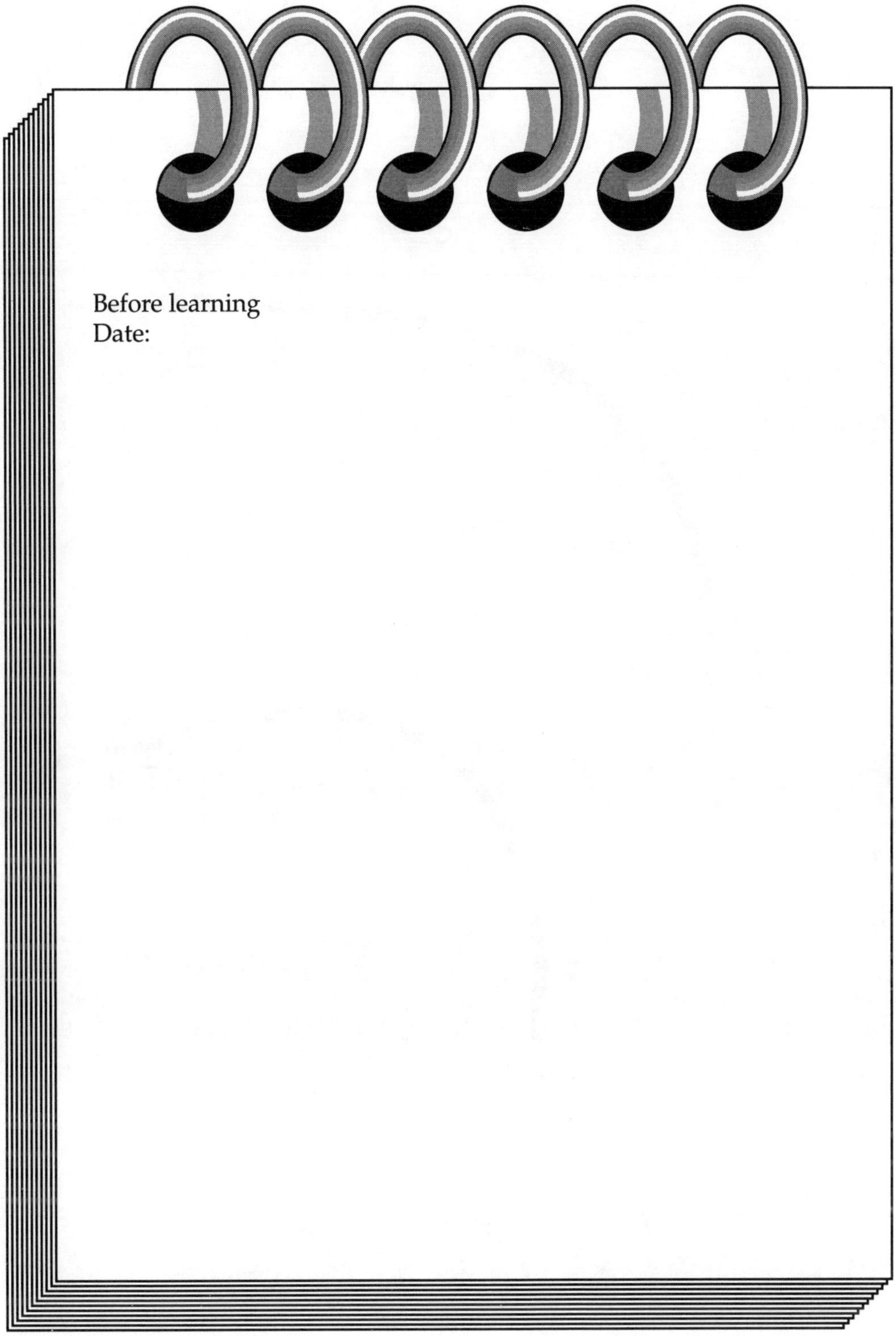

Before learning
Date:

Reproduced from *Evaluating Training*, Sharon Bartram and Brenda Gibson, Gower, Aldershot

Document 23.3 **Learning journal – your journey**

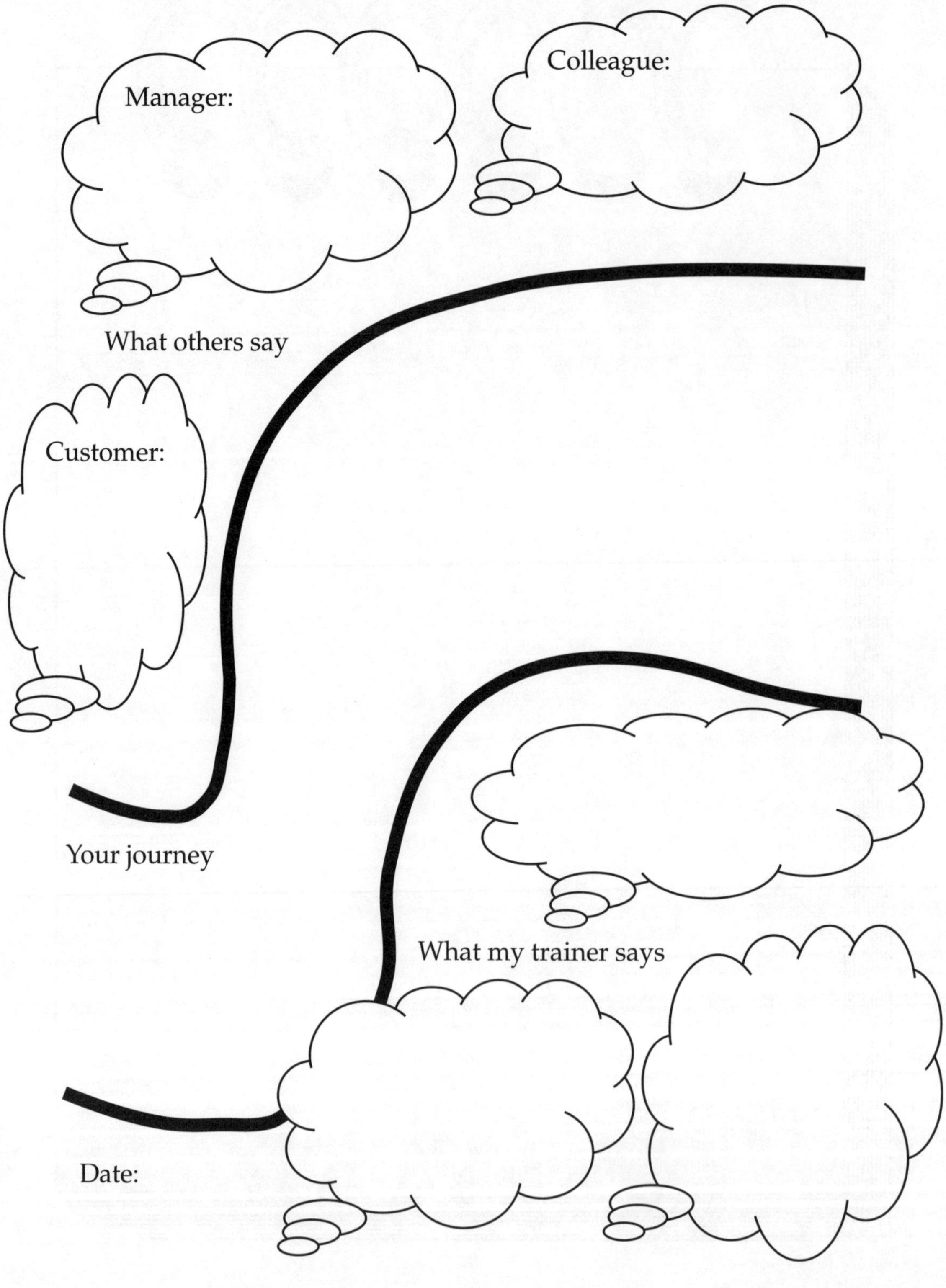

Manager:

Colleague:

What others say

Customer:

Your journey

What my trainer says

Date:

146

Reproduced from *Evaluating Training*, Sharon Bartram and Brenda Gibson, Gower, Aldershot

Learning journal – summary

Document 23.4

Summary
Date:

24

Impact questionnaire

Description
This instrument is an easy-to-complete questionnaire for measuring the impact of learning on the learners. It is appropriate for any type of training, whether in-house or external provision.

The learners complete the questionnaire about themselves in their job before the training. They repeat this process after the training and compare their responses to find out what changes and differences the training has made.

The instrument has a number of uses. It encourages the learners to take stock of their current situation and analyse this in detail. Also, the learners can develop skills of reflection and review, which can increase the impact of training as these skills give learners a greater awareness of how the training has changed them.

Adaptability
By moving the focus of the questions away from the learner, it is possible to construct a questionnaire that measures the impact of learning on departments. For example, you could ask questions about the department's level of efficiency and effectiveness, the relationship with others such as suppliers and customers.

Similarly, this technique can be adapted to measure the impact on the organization of, in particular, large-scale training initiatives. To do this you would construct questions that were more strategically oriented. For example, you might ask about goal achievement, or communicating objectives.

Timing
This instrument should be applied:

- before the training, to assess the current situation;
- at a suitable interval after the training, to identify the changes the training has brought about.

Materials
Sufficient copies of Document 24.1: Impact questionnaire.

Methods

Method description	Pros	Cons
Postal survey, using in-house methods, e.g. internal post, e-mail and follow-up interview	Easy to administer May encourage a more frank response if not face-to-face with trainer	Potentially low response rate Reticence about confidentiality
Face-to-face interview with individual learners	Can ask supplementary questions to check understanding	Time to administer May create a barrier being frank and open

Directions

1. Select your method for working with the instrument.
2. If you use a postal survey and follow-up interview, send a copy of Document 24.1 to each respondent and confirm that the replies will be dealt with in confidence. Ask the respondents to keep a copy of the questionnaire for themselves and to return a copy to you by a certain date. Agree an appropriate interval after the training and send the respondents another copy of Document 24.1 for completion. Then agree a date for a meeting to discuss with the learner both questionnaires. Ask them to compare their responses and to identify similarities and differences. Finally, together summarize from the comparison the differences the training has made.
3. You can follow a similar process if you use face-to-face interviews. Start by arranging interviews with the learners. At these interviews, introduce Document 24.1 and use the questions as a basis for discussion. Ensure that both you and the learners have a copy of the completed questionnaire at the end of the meeting. Agree a suitable interval after the training to repeat the interviews and to complete another copy of Document 24.1. Allow time at the second interview to ask the learners to compare their responses to both of their questionnaires and to identify similarities and differences. Finally, together summarize from this comparison the differences the training has made.

Consolidation

1. Review both sets of questionnaires from the learners and consider:
    - where the training has made a difference;
    - what the training has had no impact on;
    - whether the full extent of the changes from training has been realized;
    - whether more differences will become apparent over time.

2 Consider whether the changes represent a fair return on the investment made in the training.
3 Decide actions to take in the future to improve the selection of training methods as well as the quality of design and delivery.
4 Present your findings in a way that is appropriate to your circumstances, for example as a short report or as a presentation.

Document 24.1

Impact questionnaire

Title of learning:
Date(s):

Work through the following questions to help you identify the impact of the learning you have recently been involved in. You will be asked for your opinions both before and after the learning has taken place. Be as frank as you can.

1. What do you as see the purpose of the learning?

2. In terms of this purpose, how would you rate yourself in the following areas? Mark a cross (✘) on the scale to indicate your rating and add supporting comments underneath.

Confidence
Why do you say this?

LOW 1 2 3 4 5 6 7 HIGH

Knowledge
Why do you say this?

LOW 1 2 3 4 5 6 7 HIGH

Skill
Why do you say this?

LOW 1 2 3 4 5 6 7 HIGH

Ability to do the job
Why do you say this?

LOW 1 2 3 4 5 6 7 HIGH

Troubleshooting mistakes
Why do you say this?

LOW 1 2 3 4 5 6 7 HIGH

Making decisions
Why do you say this?

LOW 1 2 3 4 5 6 7 HIGH

Reproduced from *Evaluating Training*, Sharon Bartram and Brenda Gibson, Gower, Aldershot

Document 24.1 Continued

Communicating with others
Why do you say this?
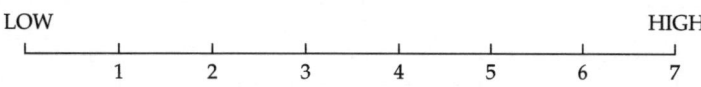

Ability to train others to do your job
Why do you say this?
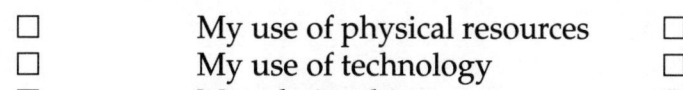

3 What aspect of your work does the learning affect? Tick all that are relevant to you.

My productivity	☐	My use of physical resources	☐
My way of working	☐	My use of technology	☐
My management of time	☐	My relationships	☐
Other (please specify)	☐		

4 How do you rate yourself against the aspects you have selected? Mark a cross (✘) on the scale to indicate your rating and write supporting comments.

Level of productivity
Why do you say this?
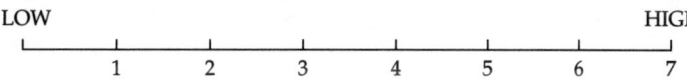

Effective way of working
Why do you say this?
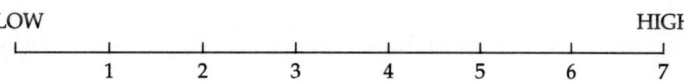

Effective use of time
Why do you say this?
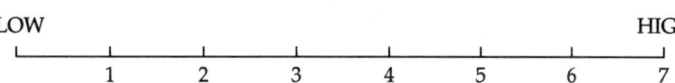

Appropriate use of physical resources
Why do you say this?
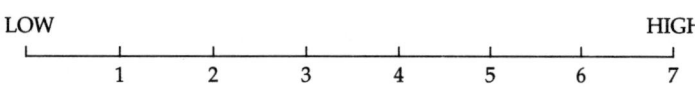

Reproduced from *Evaluating Training*, Sharon Bartram and Brenda Gibson, Gower, Aldershot

Document 24.1 Concluded

Appropriate use of technology
Why do you say this?

LOW — 1 2 3 4 5 6 7 — HIGH

Effective relationships
Why do you say this?

LOW — 1 2 3 4 5 6 7 — HIGH

Other (please specify)
Why do you say this?

LOW — 1 2 3 4 5 6 7 — HIGH

In summary, what do you think the main impact of the learning is?

Thank you for taking the time to feed back your views.

Reproduced from *Evaluating Training*, Sharon Bartram and Brenda Gibson, Gower, Aldershot

90 Brain Teasers for Trainers

Graham Roberts-Phelps and Anne McDougall

The activities and exercises in this collection are designed to broaden perception, and improve learning, thinking and problem-solving skills. Using them is also a valuable way to boost energy levels at the beginning, middle or end of any training session.

The collection will help any group engage all five senses in their learning, and develop creative and lateral thinking, word usage, mental dexterity and cooperative team skills. Most of the activities require no more than a flip chart or OHP to run. And because they need only a few moments preparation, they can be planned into sessions in advance, or simply introduced to fill gaps, or to signal a change of direction, as appropriate.

Trainers, teachers and team leaders will find *90 Brain Teasers for Trainers* a rich source of simple, flexible, and easy-to-use exercises, as well as the inspiration for their own variants.

Gower

Flip Chart Games for Trainers

Graham Roberts-Phelps

For many trainers, the flip chart is - and always will be - the simplest and most flexible instant training aid. For any line manager or team leader, working in their new role as trainer and developer, the flip chart may be the only training aid available to them. Hence this collection of *Flip Chart Games for Trainers*.

The 50 exercises, activities and games all revolve around or make active use of a flip chart. In some cases the trainer facilitates the session using the flip chart; in others, it's the participants who use it as part of the exercise. However, whether it's a short icebreaker such as *Jargon Jumble* or *Reasons to Learn*, an energizer such as *Team Talents* or a summarizing exercise such as *Cartoon Time*, or *Jigsaw*, the *Flip Chart Games for Trainers* is certain to engage the imagination and the visual sense of your participants.

Many of the games and exercises can be run in as little as 15 to 25 minutes, making them equally suitable for short meetings or extended training courses. The 'Variations' section helps you to create multiple applications for the exercises, or, if you wish, develop them into a longer training activity.

The flip chart is the essential tool for trainers and facilitators *and Flip Chart Games for Trainers* is likely to become as necessary a training aid as the flip charts themselves. A great collection for anyone wishing to inject fun, increase learning and encourage involvement in any session that they run

Gower

Team Development Games for Trainers

Roderick R Stuart

If you're involved in designing or delivering interpersonal skills training you will know that there are two perennial problems. The first is finding material that matches your objectives. The second is finding material that will be unfamiliar to the participants.

The 59 games in Roderick Stuart's collection have not appeared in print before. Based on the author's experience with a wide range of organizations and participants, they cover the entire gamut of skills associated with team development, including assertiveness, communication, creativity, decision making, influencing, listening, planning, problem solving and time management.

Each game is presented in a standard format, with an indication of objectives, timing and group size, detailed step-by-step guidance for the trainer or team leader, and ready-to-copy masters for all participants' material. An index of objectives makes it easy to select the most suitable items for your training needs and to compile complete workshops or more extensive programmes. In addition the author provides a four-stage model that relates learning to the requirements of the workplace, and a set of checklists for facilitating the learning process.

Gower